The Short Screenplay

Your Short Film from Concept to Production

Dan Gurskis

COURSE TECHNOLOGY
CENGAGE Learning™

Australia • Brazil • Japan • Korea • Mexico • Singapore • Spain • United Kingdom • United States

COURSE TECHNOLOGY
CENGAGE Learning™

The Short Screenplay:
Your Short Film from
Concept to Production
Dan Gurskis

Publisher and General Manager,
Course Technology PTR:
Stacy L. Hiquet

Associate Director of
Marketing: Sarah O'Donnell

Manager of Editorial Services:
Heather Talbot

Marketing Manager:
Mark Hughes

Executive Editor: Kevin Harreld

Marketing Coordinator:
Adena Flitt

Project Editor: Jenny Davidson

PTR Editorial Services
Coordinator: Erin Johnson

Copy Editor: Sandy Doell

Interior Layout Tech: Jill Flores

Cover Designer:
Mike Tanamachi

Indexer: Sherry Massey

For product information and
technology assistance, contact us at **Cengage Learning**
Customer & Sales Support, 1-800-354-9706

For permission to use material from this text or product,
submit all requests online at **www.cengage.com/permissions**
Further permissions questions can be emailed to
permissionrequest@cengage.com

Library of Congress Control Number: 2006906900

ISBN-13: 978-1-59863-338-2

ISBN-10: 1-59863-338-4

Course Technology
5191 Natorp Boulevard
Mason, OH 45040
USA

Cengage Learning is a leading provider of customized learning solutions with office locations around the globe, including Singapore, the United Kingdom, Australia, Mexico, Brazil, and Japan. Locate your local office at **international.cengage.com/region**

Cengage Learning products are represented in Canada by Nelson Education, Ltd.

To learn more about Course Technology, visit
www.cengage.com/coursetechnology

Purchase any of our products at your local college store or at our preferred online store **www.ichapters.com**

Printed in the United States of America
2 3 4 5 6   26 25 24 23 22

Acknowledgments

This book came about through the assistance and the encouragement of a great many people, and many thanks are due them all:

my students in the Department of Film at Brooklyn College for their honest criticism and eager support of this project from its infancy;

Michael Nolin and his students at the Savannah College of Art and Design for their constructive critiques of early drafts;

Randall Ehrmann for allowing me to include not one but two drafts of the screenplay for his excellent short film "I'm No Stud";

Vinnie Nguyen for allowing me to include so much of his developmental work on "Coming In";

Kevin Harreld for his enthusiasm in championing this project at Cengage Course Technology and Jenny Davidson for pulling it all together;

Richard Arlook of the Gersh Agency for his many years of friendship and generosity;

my talented and dedicated colleagues in the Department of Film at Brooklyn College for all their good ideas about film and teaching;

and, of course, my wonderful family—Jennifer, Emily, Teddy, and Sis.

DG

About the Author

Dan Gurskis has more than twenty years of writing and producing experience in film and television. During his career, he has worked both in this country and abroad for companies like Columbia, Paramount, RKO, HBO, Showtime, Cinemax, Comedy Central, and the USA Network, with collaborators as varied as the director Nicolas Roeg and Monty Python's Graham Chapman. In that time, he has been an Emmy Award recipient, a Cable Ace nominee, and a MacDowell Colony Fellow. For the past ten years, he has also taught screenwriting as well as lectured around the world from London to Beijing. He currently chairs the Department of Film at Brooklyn College of the City University of New York.

CONTENTS AT A GLANCE

Contents

Introduction

In 1956, Albert Lamorisse wrote the screenplay for "The Red Balloon," the classic film about the friendship between a boy and the magical balloon that he finds on the streets of Paris. The film runs 34 minutes. It contains exactly nine words of dialogue. It received an Academy Award in the category of Best Original Screenplay.

Forty years later, Kenneth Branagh wrote the screenplay for *Hamlet*. The film includes every syllable, in more or less original order, of Shakespeare's four-hour play. Branagh was nominated for an Academy Award. Shakespeare was not.

Thinking about these films, you can draw one of two conclusions. One, when it comes to screenwriting, the members of the Academy of Motion Picture Arts and Sciences are a confused lot. Or, two, there's more to screenplays and screenwriting than appearances may first suggest. (Hint: Number two is right.)

What Is a Screenplay?

At its simplest and most obvious, a screenplay is the written basis for a film. Looking for a definition that offers something more in the way of insight, many filmmakers turn to metaphor.

Some filmmakers speak of the screenplay as a road map. This is useful because it encourages people to think of film stories as journeys, literal or figurative, which they usually are.

Others speak of the screenplay as a blueprint. This architectural image is helpful because it emphasizes structure, the idea that a film is something designed and constructed.

Still others speak of the screenplay as a sales prospectus for a future product: the finished film. This somewhat mercenary view has reality on its side. Making your film requires money, and the way to acquire that money is by giving investors and benefactors a clear idea of the **story** you intend to tell and the way you intend to tell it.

> **Buzz Word**
>
> **Story:** All the underlying events of the screenplay awaiting presentation by the screenwriter. This includes even those events occurring prior to fade-in, following fade-out, and taking place off-screen (events that the screenwriter chooses not to dramatize).

Not coincidentally, each of these metaphors—road map, blueprint, prospectus—is a guide or a plan for something else, suggesting the provisional nature of the screenplay. So in defining this thing called a screenplay, you can first say that, even when the writing stops, the script is never completed in the way that a novel or a poem is.

A novelist may revise obsessively, and, even though the language and the story may improve, the work remains a collection of words, sentences, paragraphs, and chapters. The same can be said for a poet and his poem, measured in feet, lines, and stanzas.

A screenplay is different. However brilliant, it's always in a state of becoming, forever on the way to being something else—a film. You can admire a cocoon for its marriage of function and form, but ultimately it's the butterfly that will make its way in the world.

What's Important in a Screenplay?

Judging from the success of Albert Lamorisse and "The Red Balloon," dialogue isn't at the top of the list, although nearly every screenplay contains some of it and some contain a lot of it.

The relative unimportance of dialogue might surprise some audiences because dialogue is often the aspect of a film that people remember most. Who hasn't walked out of a movie theater, saying, "Wasn't that line great when she said…?" Some lines of dialogue are so memorable that they become a part of the cultural landscape. (Oh, behave!) The relative unimportance of dialogue might also surprise more than a few professional screenwriters, who regard dialogue as their one and only opportunity to communicate directly with the audience.

Alfred Hitchcock, a director who had more than a passing knowledge of film **narrative**, once said, "Dialogue should simply be a sound among other sounds, just something, that comes out of the mouths of people whose eyes tell the story in visual terms." In other words, dialogue is secondary to the main business of film: visual communication.

> **Buzz Word**
>
> **Narrative:** The process of telling a story.

This leads to the second point that you can make about this thing called a screenplay. It's primarily an exercise in visual storytelling.

But visual storytelling isn't simply a matter of shot selection and **composition**. In fact, for the screenwriter, it's anything but that. Only the most inexperienced screenwriter includes **camera directions** in a screenplay because such things are the responsibility of the director and the director of photography once the film is in production. Stories whose meaning is largely conveyed through images, and scenes whose impact is achieved within an interesting visual context, are both the core of the screenplay and the focus of the screenwriter's craft.

> **Buzz Word**
>
> **Composition:** The use of light, space, movement, and camera angle within the framed image.
>
> **Camera directions:** Directions concerning the movement of the camera as it follows the action or changes the view of the person, the object, or the scene photographed. Examples are pan, tilt, zoom, and track.

The fundamentally visual nature of film narrative has led to an interesting paradox. The screenwriter must fully imagine the film that he's writing. But—and here's where the paradox comes in—only a small part of what the screenwriter imagines should actually appear in the screenplay, which must *evoke* a sense of place and character rather than *catalogue* it down to the minutest detail. What's more, only a small part of what appears in the screenplay will ever make it to the screen in anything like its original form.

Locations, casting, performances, editing, and cinematography all conspire to create a film much different from the one that first plays in the screenwriter's head.

Smart Quote

"When I write a screenplay, I describe a movie that's already been shot."

Robert Towne, screenwriter, director

The Screenwriter's Skill Set

A novelist writes novels, a poet writes poems, a playwright writes plays, and a screenwriter writes…screens?

Well, as a matter of fact, yes. Unique among writers is the screenwriter, someone whose work has less to do with applying lessons learned in English Composition I than with translating cinematic ideas into words. To accomplish this, a screenwriter, like any writer, needs a facility with language. But that's not the most important tool in the screenwriter's toolbox.

A screenwriter must above all be a storyteller. In our world today, there are many kinds of storytellers: novelists, playwrights, journalists, songwriters, even advertising copywriters. What separates the screenwriter from the other storytellers is a clear visual sense, an understanding of the power of images, which in turn fuels the cinematic imagination.

Of course, putting a story across to an audience requires more than images alone. There must be a cohesive **plot** and compelling characters. For that, a screenwriter must have a command of screenwriting technique.

Buzz Word

Plot: The choice of events that are dramatized on-screen and the order in which they are presented.

Technique comes from a combination of talent and knowledge—knowledge of people, knowledge of narrative, knowledge of film history. Among the best ways to deepen your knowledge of film history generally and cinematic narrative specifically is to study the great films.

Unfortunately, too many aspiring filmmakers are interested in only recent films—recent American films, to be exact. This is extremely limiting, resulting in a kind of artistic inbreeding. The work of any artist in any artistic form is ultimately an amalgam of influences. The wider the sphere of influences, the more interesting the work.

Finally, screenwriters must have a collaborative spirit. Filmmaking is a partnership of a large number of people working with some fairly complex machines, and the responsibilities of each member of the production team can often be fluid. If in **blocking** a scene, for example, a director adds a line or two of dialogue not in the original screenplay, is he directing or writing? If the screenwriter creates a scene that, in its limitation of space and time, can be shot in only one way, is he writing or directing?

Buzz Word

Blocking: Arranging the positions and movements of the actors and the camera in a scene.

For professionals involved in film production, such distinctions are academic. As the screenwriter and director Robert Towne observed, "You call the writer the writer, the actor the actor, and the director the director. But they are really working together in a way that melds their respective jobs."

For a production to succeed, people do what needs to be done when it needs to be done. This takes flexibility and "film sense"—an intimate familiarity with the filmmaking process. It also takes quick-wittedness, especially when the camera is waiting to roll and egos and money are at stake. At times like these, the screenwriter must be a "down range thinker." (That's *range* as in artillery.) He must be someone who can remain composed and creative, even as the world seems to be exploding around him

As an aspiring writer, you have to ask yourself if you're truly comfortable with the layers of technology and levels of interpretation that come between the work that you do at your computer and the final product that the audience sees on the screen. If not, if you're looking for a more direct relationship with your audience, there are many forms of writing other than screenwriting that permit a one-on-one relationship. If, on the other hand, you're willing to accept the challenges unique to writing film, you'll have the opportunity to tell stories found in no other art form and at no other time in history.

Of course, you may consider yourself not only an aspiring screenwriter but also an aspiring director, producer, or cinematographer—or perhaps some combination. Well, for you, the demands of film, as well as its power, are already very clear. Still, before you can direct or produce or shoot your movie, you first need to write it.

So let's get started.

Chapter One

Shorts

"I think a story should take as long to tell as it is appropriate to that particular story."

Frank Darabont, screenwriter, director

Key Concepts

- The four categories of short films
- The characteristics of the short screenplay
- Important differences between film and theater
- Important differences between film and television

The short film is a form as old as filmmaking itself. In the early years of cinema, all films were shorts. Then, when feature films began to rise to prominence in the mid-1910s, short films continued to be popular as "short subjects" programmed on bills of double features and headlined by performers like Charlie Chaplin, Buster Keaton, and Laurel and Hardy. Eventually, though, shorts succumbed to changing economics and tastes in entertainment. By the late 1940s, only a few were made for theatrical release in the United States.

The good news is that short films are once again on the ascent. With film festivals, cable networks, specialty home video, and the Internet, there are more outlets and opportunities for screening shorts now than at any time in the last 100 years. Creating a short film for this growing audience involves many steps, none more essential than the writing of the screenplay.

It's important to understand that a short film is not simply a shorter version of a feature film any more than a short story is a shorter version of a novel or a song is a shorter version of a symphony. The way that a short film is conceptualized, written, produced, and directed is very different from that of its feature-length counterpart. What's more, the term "short film" is itself misleading, giving the impression that all films shorter than

feature-length are more alike than not. In fact, there are four distinct categories of short films, each structurally different from the others, each
determined by **running time.**

Screenwriter's Notebook: Short Films

Short-short	▪ 2-4 minutes in length
	▪ built upon a single, clear dramatic action with one crisis
	▪ usually 1-2 scenes
Conventional short	▪ 7-12 minutes in length
	▪ built upon a single, clear dramatic action with one or more crises
	▪ approximately 5-8 major scenes
Medium short	▪ 20-25 minutes in length
	▪ built upon a more complex dramatic action with multiple crises
	▪ usually underscored by a B-plot
	▪ approximately 12-15 major scenes
Long short	▪ 30 or more minutes in length
	▪ built upon a more complex dramatic action with multiple crises
	▪ underscored by a well-developed B-plot
	▪ approximately 20-30 major scenes, depending on the overall length of the screenplay

---

Notice that, as you move from one category to the next, there are gaps in
the approximate running times. For example, the maximum running time
for a short-short is four minutes, while the minimum for a conventional
short is seven minutes. The maximum for a medium short is 25 minutes,
while the minimum for a long short is 30 minutes.

Filmmaking is not engineering. A six-minute film may more closely resemble a short-short in its structure, even though its running time suggests something more complex. Similarly, a 28-minute film may make its dramatic point with only the slightest **B-plot**.

Buzz Word

A-plot: The main plot in a film that has one or more subplots. Also known as an *action line* or a *foreground line*.

B-plot: The main subplot in a film with one or more subplots. Also known as a *character line* or a *background line*.

Historically, a feature has been any film running 61 minutes or longer. Of course, you'd be hard pressed to find a feature film of that relatively brief length at your neighborhood movie house. Film distributors typically require a feature to run closer to 90 minutes, although a great many run much longer than that. Still, a 65- or 70-minute film is not legitimately a short film.

Because of the brevity of short films, an important characteristic of any successful one is an economy of expression. In a short, any short, moments must be emblematic of the larger world of the story because there's simply not enough screen time to show everything. This limitation presents some critical challenges in storytelling. It's the reason that short films, more than feature-length films, often succeed or fail at the conceptual level.

Note

Generally, one page of a screenplay will equal one minute of screen time. You can find a full discussion of screenplay form and format in Chapter 7.

The Fundamentals

As you begin to think about the short screenplay that you're going to write, you want to bear in mind several fundamental principles.

Keep your screenplay focused.

Build the plot around a single, clear dramatic **action**, which arises from a single, clear **conflict**. To do this, dramatize a pivotal moment in a character's life rather than attempting to dramatize his entire life. Creativity involves not only what you put in but also what you leave out.

Buzz Word

Action: The progressive dramatic movement of the plot.

Conflict: The fundamental opposition between characters or between a character and a dramatic force (environment, society, fate).

Limit the time frame of the action.

Aristotle and the ancient Greeks had it right: the unity of time keeps a plot from going slack. You should always compress the action of your screenplay into the briefest time period possible.

The plot for a short film should never take place over months or weeks. That would seriously diffuse dramatic tension. Ideally, the action shouldn't even take place over the course of several days. More preferable would be hours, perhaps even "real time" with the time on-screen equivalent to time in the real world.

To further increase the dramatic tension, consider some sort of time lock—a deadline by which something must be accomplished or the conflict must be resolved. There's a reason that every detonating device in a Hollywood action movie has a digital readout, counting down the minutes to the explosion. Deadlines add tension. They force people to act—*now*.

Limit the number of characters.

An audience connects with a film through its characters. Not only will an audience fail to identify with a large cast of characters in a short amount of screen time, it may have difficulty just telling them apart. In a film that's two or three minutes long, for example, three characters are almost too many.

Visualize.

The writer and philosopher Johann Wolfgang von Goethe observed that all art is superficial. It draws meaning and depth from working with surfaces. The world's greatest visual art—"Mona Lisa," "Starry Night"—occurs in only two dimensions. Film is no less superficial. It's the art of telling a story through images—moving images. The challenge lies in mining what is beneath the surface and finding a visual equivalent for it, transforming the mental into the physical, the internal into the external.

Say more with less.

When images alone can't express meaning, dialogue is used as a complement. But keep in mind that a competent actor can say more with his face in a close-up than a superb screenwriter can say in pages of dialogue. Also keep in mind that a script that is entirely dialogue-driven is better suited to television or theater than film.

Make it new.

Each person's life is a unique accumulation of experiences. You must draw upon that uniqueness to create a screenplay that you alone can write. Only then will you write something that's truly new. At the same time, newness isn't simply novelty, so never pursue it for its own sake. In a short film, everything down to the smallest detail must have a dramatic purpose.

What to Avoid

Just as important as doing the right thing is not doing the wrong thing. Some ideas are simply unsuited for short films, and no amount of writing or directing talent will change that.

The extensive use of special or visual effects

As good as desktop editing and effects software has become, it's still not as powerful as what the major movie studios have at their disposal. No matter how much talent you have, you can't make *The Lord of the Rings* as a five-minute film with a budget of one hundred dollars.

Buzz Word

Special effects: Those effects—rain, snow, explosions, firearms hits—created live on the set.

Visual effects: Effects added in post-production by manipulating the recorded image.

Multiple subplots

As challenging as it is to keep many characters straight, keeping many subplots straight is harder. Even in a long short of 30 minutes or more, a main plot and one subplot will provide more than enough events to sustain audience interest.

Other ideas are unsuited for short films simply because audiences have seen some variation of them too many times before. Thousands of shorts are made every year, and an equal number of short screenplays are written in search of directors and producers. For a work to gain serious attention, it must cut through what advertising and marketing executives call "clutter." It must be original.

Here are some things to avoid so that your work doesn't disappear into the black hole of clutter.

Resolution through death (either murder or suicide)

While death certainly brings resolution to a story, more often than not it results from a poverty of imagination rather than a compelling dramatic purpose. Killing off a character is never a particularly inventive plot development.

Weapons

Just as death is an easy resolution, a pistol pointed at someone's head is an easy motivator. What's more, weapons present certain production issues (something that will be dealt with in Chapter 6).

Serial killing

The specificity of this kind of death doesn't make it any more original or appealing. In fact, serial killers are about as overdone as characters can possibly be.

Parodies and mockumentaries

From *Blazing Saddles* to *A Mighty Wind*, parodies and mockumentaries have made for some extremely funny films. In writing a screenplay like this, though, a screenwriter is expressing more about the original than about himself. Even if you're extraordinarily clever, there won't be much new in what you write. Make your work your own.

Buzz Word

Parody: Any work of art that copies another work of art in a deliberate, comic, and satirical way.

Mockumentary: A mock documentary, usually comic in nature.

Dreams and fantasies

Establishing a convincing world in your screenplay will invariably take more screen time than you expect. Neither dream sequences nor fantasy sequences contribute to the creation of that world. In fact, they detract from it. Just as bad, they are clichés. Who hasn't seen a dream sequence so disturbing to a character that it causes him to wake up panting and sweating at the thought of it? Who hasn't seen that *many* times?

Characters who are obviously walking contradictions

The prostitute with the heart of gold, the kindly homeless man, the Gandhi-quoting soldier, the mentally disturbed individual who speaks great truths despite the fact that he's otherwise incapable of rational thought—if the contradiction is that obvious, someone has thought of it long before you. So, in addition to lacking authenticity, it lacks originality.

Screenwriter's Notebook: Conceptualizing the Short Screenplay

Yes	No
Focused action	Multiple subplots
Limited time frame	Elaborate effects
Limited number of characters	Resolution through death
Visual storytelling	Serial killers
Originality	Weapons
Emotional authenticity	Mockumentaries and parodies
	Dreams and fantasies

Film and Theater

To understand the way a screenplay works, you must understand, first, the way film works and, second, the way it works differently from other forms of dramatic performance.

True, on a simplistic level, film and theater are similar. Both are interpretative. The writer doesn't speak directly to the audience, relying instead on actors, directors, and designers to present and enhance (and sometimes distort) the meaning of the written text. The overall structure of plays and screenplays also shares certain common elements: character, conflict, and dramatic action. There, the similarity ends.

Smart Quote

"Compare the cinema with theatre. Both are dramatic arts. Theatre brings actors before a public and every night during the season they re-enact the same drama. Deep in the nature of theatre is a sense of ritual. The cinema, by contrast, transports its audience individually, singly, out of the theatre towards the unknown."

John Berger, critic

In a very real sense, the play's the thing. It endures even after the theater has emptied, even after a production has closed. It has a life of its own, ready for any number of future productions.

A screenplay, on the other hand, exists only to be filmed—once. Unlike stage plays, screenplays are not studied as literature, and the reason is simple: the primacy of the medium is the finished film rather than the script that inspires it. The art, in other words, is in the execution.

The playwright Edward Albee has said, "A production is nothing more than an opinion about a play. It may be true, it may be half-true, or it may be a total lie." A production of a film isn't an opinion about the screenplay. The screenplay is an opinion about the production.

This distinction stems from basic differences in expression in the two dramatic forms. Film is fundamentally visual, theater fundamentally verbal. A stage director may block a scene of a play to highlight a moment or an action. A lighting designer may reinforce the stage picture. But what's spoken remains the essence of the experience. That the words can and probably will be spoken in many different ways by many different actors suggests that theater is about reinterpretation as much as interpretation.

A well-written play, though primarily intended for performance, may even speak as eloquently to someone reading it in an easy chair as it does to someone seated in the balcony. In comparison, a screenplay's half-life as a reading experience is either brief or irrelevant, depending on whether it leads to the production of a film or a quick toss into the trash can.

The Writer's Goals

Smart Quote

"In the theater, while you recognized that you were looking at a house, it was a house in quotation marks. On screen, the quotation marks tend to be blotted out by the camera."

Arthur Miller, playwright

Ultimately, the goals of screenwriter and playwright are as divergent as the dramatic forms in which they work. By and large, a playwright uses the play to investigate character and **theme**. The story, such as it is, generally serves these twin interests. A screenwriter aims for something like the opposite. The focus of the screenplay is usually—although certainly not always—the story. Character and theme function in service of it. This is true even in a character-centered screenplay, which still tends to be story-driven.

Buzz Word

Theme: The ultimate meaning of a work derived from the characters, the actions that they take, and the consequences of those actions.

To achieve their differing goals, the playwright and the screenwriter have at their disposal tools and conventions specific to their respective dramatic forms. The use of space in the theater, for example, is strikingly different from the use of space in film. On stage, space represents a poetic suggestion of an imagined reality. A bench may be just a bench, but it may also represent a seat on a subway train, a throne, or the peak of Mt. Everest. While the three-dimensionality of stage space is sometimes framed by a **proscenium** arch, the two-dimensionality of film space is always framed, and within that frame is a literal depiction of an imagined reality.

Buzz Word

Proscenium: The wall that separates the stage from the auditorium in a theater.

In Focus: The Representational Image

In film, reality may be as fantastic as the inner earth of *The Lord of the Rings* or as futuristic as the death star of *Star Wars*, but the images remain representational rather than poetic. They are what they are. They require no additional imagining by the audience to understand their meaning.

Even the most minutely **naturalistic** set requires the **suspension of disbelief** by the audience watching the play performed. In fact, attending a play is in itself an act of imagination. The performance is live, and the presence of an audience affects it, shading the meaning of the text and creating a connection between actor and spectator.

Buzz Word

Naturalistic: Imitating reality in an exact and faithful way.

Suspension of disbelief: The ability to repress the knowledge that a film or a play is only an invention and to respond to dramatic events as if they are real.

Watching a film, on the other hand, is a more passive experience because technology mediates the viewing in several important ways.

First, unlike a play, a film is unchanging once it arrives in a theater. Whether the audience is cheering enthusiastically or hooting derisively, the action on the screen unfolds in the same way each and every time.

Second, the insistence on **verisimilitude** in film—that is, the tendency toward creating a literal reality on the screen—leaves little within the frame for the audience to imagine.

Buzz Word

Verisimilitude: The appearance of being real or true.

Third, shot composition and editing choices shape the content of the frame in such a way as to direct the interest of the viewer.

Still, any limitation on the imaginative participation of the audience is more than offset by those methods of visual expression unique to film. There are no **close-ups** or **montages** in the theater, no **tracking shots** or visual effects. It's precisely these devices and techniques that allow for the breadth of expression that audiences expect from film. For an audience to have its interest manipulated by a talented filmmaker is not a bad thing. Under the right circumstances, it may be a truly memorable experience.

Buzz Word

Close-up: A shot that provides a magnified view of a character or an object.

Montage: Although there are many forms of montage, the term is most commonly used to describe a technique in which a series of shots is edited together to suggest in a short period of time the essence of events occurring over a longer period of time.

Tracking shot: A shot in which the camera and its mount are moved.

While the theater is a more immediate experience for the audience, it places greater limitation on the creative team staging the production. Contemporary economics dictate smaller casts and single-unit sets for all but the most lavish Broadway shows.

In deciding whether to go to the theater or to the movies, then, you seem to have a choice between creative limitation for the audience (film) or creative limitation for the production (stage).

Screenwriter's Notebook: Theater and Film Compared

Theater	Film
Focus is on language	Focus is on images
Written text is primary	Finished film is primary
Space is abstract or poetic	Space is framed and literal
Performance is direct to the audience	Performance is mediated by technology
Performance is heightened	Performance is intimate
Audience is active	Audience is passive
Story serves character and theme	Theme and character serve the story
Ephemeral (when the curtain falls, the experience remains only in memory)	Lasting (the experience is preserved on celluloid, tape, or disc)

The Script

What's on the page differs greatly in plays and screenplays. Although some playwrights like George Bernard Shaw and Eugene O'Neill write stage directions almost novelistic in their detail, most playwrights use dialogue alone to create characters, convey theme, and advance plot. Theatrical dialogue is more stylized than film dialogue, often employing devices like **monologue** and **soliloquy**, sometimes even appearing in verse form. Stage directions range from functional to nearly nonexistent.

> **Buzz Word**
>
> **Monologue:** A long speech by a single actor.
>
> **Soliloquy:** A monologue intended to give the impression of unspoken thoughts or feelings. Sometimes referred to as an *interior monologue*.

Screenwriters, on the other hand, depend on **scene directions** more than dialogue to suggest the cinematic possibilities of a story. To make the internal external, one of the critical responsibilities of their work, they depict action that reveals the thoughts and the emotions of their characters. Dialogue tends to be spare, consisting of brief speeches usually no more than a line or two in length.

> **Buzz Word**
>
> **Scene directions:** The description of characters, locations, and physical action found in the screenplay. Sometimes referred to as *action, stage directions,* or *description*.

Over the years, there has been increasingly less overlap in the respective skill sets of screenwriters and playwrights. At the beginning of the sound era in motion pictures, playwrights were routinely lured from the theater and brought to Hollywood to work as screenwriters. Today, the more likely move is from the theater into television. With its emphasis on character-centered, dialogue-driven stories, television drama is closer to theater than to film in its storytelling technique.

Television does share some outward similarities with film, and, as television dramas become visually more sophisticated, the similarities seem to grow. The reality, however, is that there is less than meets the eye.

Film and Television

Television began its history as essentially radio with pictures. The performers, the genres, even the shows themselves were adapted from radio to the fledgling medium with little modification. Television introduced a camera to perform for and a set to perform on, but otherwise the underlying storytelling technique of radio remained largely unchanged.

In a fundamental way, the medium has never really outgrown its roots: there's still not much vision in television. The focus continues to be on dialogue, and characters speak more, not less, in contemporary television programs. Scripts for hour-long dramas, which once were 44 or 45 pages, now sometimes run 65 or 70 pages. The shows are not longer; the actors simply speak faster—much faster.

Smart Quote

"Television does not dominate or insist, as movies do.... For most of us, it is something turned on and off as we would the light. It is a service, not a luxury or a thing of choice."

David Thomson, film historian

Yes, many contemporary dramatic series are built around an interesting look or striking visual effects, but the stories are still told exclusively through dialogue. The visual elements of these programs may delight the eye, but they don't propel the action. This is as true on premium cable channels like HBO and Showtime as it is on the commercial networks. Sitcoms, aside from the occasional sight gag, have no visual elements whatsoever. Not surprisingly, scripts for television programs, like those for the theater, consist almost entirely of dialogue with only the barest of scene directions on the page. And so television's lack of visual emphasis is built into the writing process.

Even when an important piece of information is communicated visually in television, it's almost always commented upon by at least one character, whose dialogue reinforces or restates the information conveyed through the image. There are two reasons for this, both extremely practical.

First, the size of the television screen varies widely from household to household and room to room. While one viewer may be watching a show on a plasma screen television in a media room, another may be watching it on a nine-inch portable in the kitchen. The content of a shot that is adequately clear on a large screen might be barely discernible on a smaller one.

Second, television producers have traditionally been leery of the attention span of their audience. Unlike plays or films, which require their audiences to make a deliberate choice to attend and then to spend money, time, and energy once they have, television is a medium that comes to its audience, wherever the audience may be. And so television viewing is often done in tandem with some other activity: reading the newspaper, making a sandwich, disciplining the family pet.

If critical information is communicated solely through images while a television viewer is even partially distracted, there's the possibility that the story will become unclear for that person. A lack of clarity leads to confusion, which may encourage the viewer to change the channel, the death knell for any television program.

In a way that images do not, dialogue allows television writers to make certain that all viewers have access to the same story information. To reinforce dialogue, television editors often edit scenes so that the camera is directed at the character speaking, eliminating reaction shots almost entirely. Not only do viewers *hear* the characters speaking, but they also *see* them speaking.

Smart Quote

"Television…helps blur the distinction between framed and unframed reality. Whereas going to the movies necessarily entails leaving one's ordinary surroundings, soap operas are in fact spatially inseparable from the rest of one's life."

Eviatar Zerubavel, sociologist, educator

While the predominance of "talking heads" is unmistakable in television, no less important is the role of time constraints. In broadcast television, time is paramount, and every show—drama, comedy, or made-for-television movie—is written with a time limit in mind. Sitcoms currently have 21–22 minutes of actual program, dramas 42–44 minutes, and made-for-television movies 84–88 minutes. Even when there are not 44 minutes of story in a script, there will still need to be 44 minutes of television program (and that's exactly 44 minutes, not a split-second over or under).

Shows on premium cable channels and public television have more leeway, but they are not totally without limits. An episode of *The Sopranos*, for example, can't come in at 58 minutes one week and 21 the next.

The preciseness of these time constraints presents a challenge for writers and producers. Scripts that run short are padded with establishing shots and **drive-ups**. Scripts that run long are winnowed to their essentials. With all but the most crucial moments gone, a great deal of cutting from interior to interior occurs without even a passing nod in the direction of visual variety.

Perhaps the most recognized feature of television is the commercial break—or, as it's euphemistically called, "the station break." Obviously, television programs on premium cable networks and public television don't have to contend with this particular constraint. All others, though, must be structured to accommodate a commercial interruption every seven or eight minutes. As a cynic once noted, "Television shows exist to separate the commercials."

What results is a story plotted with numerous climaxes, many of them false, which spike the action just before a commercial interruption. These climaxes mean to entice viewers to keep their fingers off the remote control and to stay with the program, no matter how long and no matter how many the commercials may be. Hour-long television shows tend to have even greater climaxes—cliffhangers—on the half-hour, midway through the program, when the commercial break is usually several minutes longer than the breaks nearer the quarter-hour.

In and of themselves, the creative limitations of television are not particularly relevant to writing film. Their importance lies in the sheer number of hours that most aspiring filmmakers have spent in front of a television set. Even screenwriters who consider themselves serious students of cinema see very few films relative to the number of television shows that they have watched.

This means that, simply from their viewing habits, they will more likely have internalized the principles of television storytelling technique rather than those of cinematic storytelling technique. Because the superficial similarities between film and television are even greater than those between film and theater, this internalization process becomes that much more difficult to counteract when someone sets out to write a screenplay.

Now that you have an overview of the short screenplay, it's time to get down to specifics. Since Aristotle, writers and critics have debated the relative importance of character versus story. Does a story determine the characters or do the characters determine the story? The truth is that in film character and story are inextricably linked. Each affects the other in an ongoing give and take. Still, for a screenwriter writing a short screenplay, the best way to begin the creative process is by thinking about character.

Chapter One, Take Two—Chapter Review

A short film is not simply a shorter version of a feature film. The way that short films are conceptualized, written, produced, and directed is very different from feature films.

There are four main categories of short films:

- Short-short (2-4 minutes in length)
- Conventional short (7-12 minutes in length)
- Medium short (20-25 minutes in length)
- Long short (30 minutes or longer)

Each is structurally different from the others.

In conceptualizing your short screenplay, you should keep in mind some important principles:

- Limit the time frame of the action.
- Limit the number of characters.
- Make your screenplay visual.
- Say more with less—that goes for dialogue, pages, and even entire scenes.
- Be original.

In conceptualizing your screenplay, you should also be careful to avoid certain things:

- The extensive use of special or visual effects
- Large casts
- Multiple subplots
- Story resolution through death (either murder or suicide)
- Weapons
- Serial killers
- Parodies and mockumentaries
- Dreams and fantasies
- Characters who are obviously walking contradictions

Theater differs from film in its reliance on stylized language, heightened performance styles, and the non-literal use of space.

Television differs from film in its reliance on dialogue-driven dramatic action and time-determined plots.

Chapter Two

CHARACTER

"I consider every film to be a biography, regardless of whether it's a biography of a living person or a fictitious person.

Milos Forman, screenwriter, director

Key Concepts

- Character vs. characterization
- The five aspects of character: objective, need, outlook, attitude, arc
- The four main types of characters

In traditional cinematic narrative, character is the primary way that a film engages an audience. If the audience identifies with one or more of the main characters in the film, there will likely be a connection with the events on-screen because the audience is invested in what happens. If there's no identification, a connection will be less likely.

For any audience identification to occur, a character must be empathetic. Empathy is not the same as sympathy. Empathy is, first, the understanding that an audience has for a character's feelings and actions and, second, the concern that comes out of that understanding.

Sympathy, on the other hand, is the audience's shared feelings with a character—that is, the audience and the character have an identical emotional response. Certain film genres depend on a sympathetic, almost visceral response from the audience. The goal of a horror film, for example, is to frighten the audience as thoroughly as its on-screen victims. Yet, for most films, sympathy is not crucial. Empathy always is.

Smart Quote

"The cinema makes it possible to experience without danger all the excitement, passion and desirousness which must be repressed in a humanitarian ordering of life."

Carl Jung, psychiatrist and founder of analytical psychology

Sometimes, the process of identification with a character is complex, involving more than empathy or sympathy alone. The character may provide a vicarious experience of the forbidden, a way for the audience to live through dangerous or illegal activities without actually taking part in them. Audiences often identify with **antiheroes** in this way. Similarly, a character may represent a fantasy that, although not particularly dangerous, the audience would still be unwilling or unable to play out in life. Love stories, whether comic or serious, draw on this element of fantasy in connecting with an audience.

Buzz Word

Antihero: A character that evokes audience identification even though he's not brave, noble, good, or otherwise heroic in nature. Antiheroes are typically outlaws or characters on the fringes of society.

While character is important in any film, it's especially important in a short film because of the various narrative and technical limitations inherent in the form. Without splashy effects or an overly elaborate plot, the short film must look inward. As a result, an effective short screenplay is almost always character-centered.

Character and Characterization

Character should not be confused with characterization, which consists of the observable qualities and traits of an individual. These qualities and traits can be social, psychological, or physical. They are the dimensions referred to in the phrase "three-dimensional character."

With the exception of gender and age, physical traits are largely unimportant in a screenplay. The reason is basic. Eventually, your screenplay will become a film, and an actor will inhabit the role that you write. Unless there's some unique physical trait that determines the direction of the story, you'll cast the most talented actor available rather than the one who most closely resembles the physical type that you originally had in mind for the role.

Screenwriter's Notebook: Character Traits and Qualities	
Dimension	**Traits/Qualities**
Social	Religious beliefs
	Economic class
	Ethnicity
	Political views
Psychological	Temperament
	Intelligence
	Psyche
	Moral values
Physical	Gender
	Age
	Race
	Physique

To deepen their understanding of their cast of characters, screenwriters will sometimes write a detailed biography for each one before beginning work on a screenplay. (Actors like to do something similar.) If this exercise helps you, by all means use it. You'll be in good company.

No matter how detailed the biography, though, you'll still be dealing with characterization rather than character. Like traits and qualities, biographical data does not reveal the essence of a character. As many a successful person has demonstrated, the facts of a life are less important than what someone does with them.

Ultimately, a character is defined by the choices made during the course of the screenplay's action. A choice naturally involves a decision. But the decision is in the doing, not in the consideration of what should be done. In other words, a choice is active and external. Something happens—something that the audience can see.

Smart Quote

"What is character but the determination of incident? And what is incident but the illumination of character?"

Henry James, novelist

Why Are Character Choices Active and External?

Sad but true, in our society today, we have come to distrust what people say. Part of that has to do with the white lies that we tell in the name of civility. If, for example, a friend who is looking a little plump asks, "Am I fat?", you automatically respond, "Not at all." When your sister arrives at the door with a date who seems to have spent the better part of his life in lockup at San Quentin, you politely smile and say, "What an interesting guy."

Although this lack of candor has become an accepted part of civilized behavior, it does foster skepticism about virtually every social exchange. As the playwright George Bernard Shaw wrote, "The liar's punishment is not in the least that he is not believed, but that he cannot believe anyone else."

Beyond simple civility, though, is something more insidious. In the contemporary world with clergymen involved in sex scandals, corporate executives involved in financial scandals, and elected officials involved in political scandals, it sometimes seems that any public figure not lying is at the very least spinning the truth.

Audiences seem to have assimilated this fact of modern life into a cynical view of all speech, including its dramatic form: dialogue. Consequently, they often distrust what a character says, especially if the statement is direct and significant. The only reliable information, then, comes from what a character does. "Show," as the often quoted saying goes, "don't tell."

For any choice to reveal character, it must have consequences—dramatic consequences. Something must be at stake for either the character or the world of the story. If nothing is at stake, then no true dramatic choice exists.

Thrillers, horror films, and action films are popular with audiences for a reason. What happens on-screen is a matter of life and death. What better way to know and to identify with a character than to observe him in this caldron? And, if the character is sympathetic, what better way to experience the thrill of cheating death?

> **In Focus: Dramatic Choice**
>
> A character's decision concerning what to eat for breakfast or what to wear to the office is not a true dramatic choice. There are no real consequences to a choice between oatmeal and a banana nut muffin or the blue pinstriped suit and the double-breasted blazer. A true dramatic choice must have the potential to alter the life of the character or the world of the story in some way.

Logically, the most revealing choice is one that holds the greatest consequences. Because of the way narrative films are structured, the most important choice that a character can make occurs in the climax. It's here that the main problem of the story is resolved and the **major dramatic question** is answered, giving any choice its greatest weight.

Buzz Word

Major dramatic question: The central problem of the screenplay expressed in the form of a question. For example, the major dramatic question in a love story is usually very simple: will the boy get the girl?

Minor dramatic question: The problem of the B-plot expressed in the form of a question. For example, in a romantic comedy in which the B-plot focuses on the lovers' feuding sets of parents, the minor dramatic question would be, will the parents patch up their differences for the sake of their children?

Next in importance is the choice made at the beginning of the film because it sets the plot into motion. All other choices will vary in importance but never surpass those at the opening and the closing of the action.

Note

In a short-short, because of the sheer brevity of the plot, the first choice is sometimes made prior to fade-in. The film then opens with the consequences of that choice.

Putting Your Characters in Charge of the Action

So how do you put a character in the position to make choices that will propel the action? First, keep in mind that a character is essentially an idea rather than a person. He's a force in the story, existing to push the action forward and to be pushed in turn. This is as true of the **protagonist** as it is of the **antagonist** or any secondary character that may appear.

Buzz Word

Protagonist: The character that drives the action of the story.

Antagonist: The character that presents the main opposition to the protagonist as that character pursues his objective.

To "know a character" really means to understand the effect that he has on the action and the effect that the action has on him. And for a character to make choices that affect the action in some meaningful way, he must want something. He must have an **objective**.

Buzz Word

Objective: A goal that motivates a character's choices and actions. An objective is sometimes referred to as a *want*.

An objective can be expressed in a single, straightforward sentence, and it relates specifically to the plot. In *Romeo and Juliet* by William Shakespeare, Romeo's objective is to keep alive the love of Juliet. (Theirs is a love at first sight, so winning her love isn't truly an issue.) In the story, Romeo isn't seeking happiness or fulfillment or even romance in some broad way, although clearly Juliet's love might lead to all those. It's Juliet he wants, and it's this objective that drives the action.

This brings up an important point. In their generality, fundamental human desires are no objective at all. You can safely say that most people seek love, friendship, and respect in life, even though there have been films made about characters who clearly don't. If your character pursues any of these generalized "life goals," you'll find yourself struggling to make him come alive for an audience, as empathetic as he may otherwise be. An objective that lacks specificity leads to character choices that lack specificity, which do little to engage an audience.

Of course, a character seeking the affection or attention of another character—as in the case of Romeo—is an entirely different matter. Here, the goal isn't affection generally but the affections of one character in particular. This puts a finer point on what could be an overly broad pursuit. Not only is the objective specific, but something like it is the basis for virtually every romantic comedy and drama ever written.

In Focus: Objectives

In "Life Lessons," a segment in the short film trilogy *New York Stories*, Lionel Dobie, a prominent New York artist, wants to prevent his young assistant Paulette from quitting her job with him and moving out of his loft. That is Lionel's objective: to keep his assistant from leaving him. In the course of the 44-minute film, he does a great many things, some funny, some sad, some cruel, and some outrageous. All arise from that single objective.

A man of Lionel's age and stature would have a wide range of desires. He might want to hold onto his fame. He might want to enhance his artistic reputation. He might want to attain immortality in some way. He might even be searching for peace of mind. Despite the fact that each of these represents a desire of some kind, none is legitimately an objective. Why? They are not specific enough to the plot to motivate the character in his choices and to move the action forward.

While a generalized objective is problematic, one that's vague or unformed is worse. Simply put, a character without a clear objective will frustrate an audience. Think of it. Why would any reasonable moviegoer spend time watching someone whose chief activity is floundering? There's enough of that in life. Why suffer through it in a film?

Yes, there are films about alienated, directionless characters, but often their attitude masks an objective that emerges as the action progresses and the character reveals his true nature. If you want the audience on your character's side, you need a reason for it: a strong and clear objective.

Merely having an objective isn't enough, though. A character must be prepared to act, to pursue the objective. Unless he has the will to succeed, there's no cause for action. You and I may yearn for wealth or fame or popularity, but, unless we have the determination to go after it, we're engaging in idle talk and nothing more. The same is true for a character.

Just as important as willfulness is opportunity: a character must have a credible chance of attaining an objective. If a character wants something but has absolutely no way of getting it, where's the story? The action will essentially be an exercise in futility, which will become very boring very quickly. The audience must believe that there's at least an outside possibility that the character will realize his objective. At the same time, the objective shouldn't be so easy to attain that pursuing it presents no serious challenge to the character. An objective that involves difficulty creates drama.

Of course, just because a character wants something doesn't mean that he'll get it, no matter how strong the character and no matter how clear the objective. As in life, some get what they want, and others don't. Whether the pursuit of an objective ultimately succeeds or fails, it often brings focus to a more serious concern for a character: **need**.

Buzz Word
___

Need: A character's subconscious desire or unacknowledged emotional want.

Objective and Need

Although an objective is critical in defining who a character is and what he will do, truly compelling characters connect with an audience on more than one level. An objective deals with the surface of a character's desires. Underlying that surface is a need.

Like an objective, a need motivates choices and actions. But it does so in ways that a character doesn't fully understand. In fact, because a need involves unarticulated desires, a character may never be completely aware of it, even by fade-out. What makes a need so critical is that it represents a problem that requires resolving or a situation that demands changing. Something must be done about it, or the character's world will forever remain out of balance.

The relationship between need and objective varies significantly from screenplay to screenplay. In some screenplays, an objective and a need may complement each other. A character may want what he needs, and he may need what he wants. In other screenplays, an objective and a need may contradict each other. A character may want something and pursue it vigorously, even though he really needs just the opposite. When a character's objective and need are at odds with each other, there is an **internal conflict**.

Buzz Word

Internal conflict: A form of conflict pitting a character's objective against his need.

Note

A more in-depth discussion of conflict can be found in the next chapter.

A common storytelling technique is to use the pursuit of a character's objective to expose his need. Then, rather than realize his objective, he satisfies his need in the course of the action.

For example, a musician is struggling to make a hit record because he wants fame and fortune in the music business. In reality, though, he needs a soul mate to bring stability to his life and to add meaning to his music. Here, a typical resolution might be for the musician to fail commercially but succeed romantically—to lose the record deal but win the woman—and become a better person and a better musician for it.

Does every character have an objective? Yes. Does every character have a need? Well, minor characters may not, especially if they appear only in passing. Central characters in a short-short also may not, simply because there's not enough screen time for that degree of psychological depth. However, the longer the film and the greater the complexity of the characters, the likelier there will be a need for a need.

In Focus: Objective vs. Need

Here's an easy way to distinguish between objective and need. If you were able to enter the world of a story and question a character, he would be able to tell you what he wants (his objective), although not what he lacks emotionally and psychologically (his need).

Adding Depth to Your Characters

Because the most compelling characters are often the most complex, a screenwriter must provide characters with as much depth as possible. Objective and need clearly contribute to this. Characterization does not. But there are other aspects of character that can add depth and enrich complexity.

Outlook is the way a character views the world.

A character may have an outlook that is naïve or cynical, trusting or suspicious, optimistic or pessimistic—the possibilities are endless. But an outlook is more than a trait or a quality. It's central to the character, influencing choices and actions. The way a character sees the world will go a long way toward determining the way he acts in the world.

Yes, outlook may reflect an objective or a need—that is, a character may look at the world in a certain way because of what he wants or what he needs. Still, it remains a distinct and important aspect of its own.

A character's ability to identify his outlook is directly related to his self-awareness. Like people, some characters have yet to discover that they are cynics or romantics or whatever, while others revel in the knowledge of who they honestly are.

Attitude is the way the world views a character.

Every character presents himself to the world in some identifiable way, often without ever realizing that he's doing it. Attitude involves not only this presentation but also the response to it by others.

Attitude is different from temperament, which is a quality. Like outlook, it may reflect an objective or a need. Unlike outlook, it's external, something for all to see.

Because attitude is important in putting a character's actions into context, it should never be one note played over and over again. If a character has the attitude of a bully, for example, he shouldn't bully every person that he meets, which would be repetitive and eventually just plain silly. He should have, though, an aggressiveness that can surface at any time.

Similarly, if a character has a world-weary attitude, he shouldn't be bored and indifferent to everything that happens around him. Instead, becoming engaged by people and events may take more time and effort for him.

Ultimately, attitude is a framework. Within that framework, the screenwriter should aim for as much variety and subtlety as possible.

Objective, need, outlook, and attitude are all predictors of behavior. Objective and need indicate what a character can do. Outlook and attitude indicate how the character can do it. What results from these predictors are choices and actions, and what results from those choices and actions is change.

Arc is the growth or the change that a character undergoes during the course of the film's action.

Narrative film is about change. The world of the story is somehow different at fade-out than it was at fade-in. For this transformation to occur, the protagonist must either undergo change or cause change in others. A character that accomplishes neither will frustrate the audience because, without change, the action of the film is essentially pointless. And if a film has no point, even a light or humorous one, why turn on the projector in the first place?

It's unusual that a protagonist does not change at all, even when his main purpose is to cause change in others. A character that remains the same, even if he is actively pursuing an objective, is not a particularly interesting thing to watch. Character arc—a change undergone by any character, protagonist or otherwise—is the dramatic movement from one emotional, psychological, or social state to another, different state.

In a short screenplay, finding an appropriate arc is essential. A character can't go from absolute evil to absolute good in ten minutes. The audience won't accept so complete a transformation in so short a time because it contradicts what people know about human nature: any change takes time; significant change takes a long time. So in a short screenplay with its limited time frame, only a moderate or minimal change is credible.

For the most convincing arc, a character should be inclined to change even before the action of the screenplay begins. If he's going to quit his job in the climax, for instance, he should be desperately unhappy with it at fade-in. If he's going to marry his fiancée in the resolution, the wedding plans should have already been set before page one.

Audiences connect with characters in dynamic situations. Suggesting the potential for change early in the action allows the audience to make that connection quickly. The sooner an audience is connected to a story, the likelier it will remain so all the way to fade-out.

Screenwriter's Notebook: Aspects of Character

Objective	The goal that motivates a character's actions and choices
Need	A character's subconscious yearning or unacknowledged emotional want
Outlook	The way the character views the world
Attitude	The way the world views a character
Arc	The transformation that a character undergoes during the course of the action

---

In Focus: Circular Stories

A favorite strategy among novice screenwriters is to create stories that begin and end at the same point. A character starts the story destitute and hopeless, strikes it rich, and then through some stroke of bad luck, ends the story destitute and homeless. Often, these are slice-of-life stories. Avoid them. Screenplays with circular stories have been around for a long time. They are all too familiar to everyone but the screenwriters who write them.

Types of Characters

Characters serve very specific dramatic functions, and it's by these functions that they are defined. The protagonist is that character whose objective, choices, and actions drive the story. Sometimes, this character is referred to as the hero. Unfortunately, this terminology implies something about the inner nature of the character, suggesting that he is noble or brave or honorable, which may not turn out to be true.

A protagonist may possess heroic qualities, but whether he does is entirely irrelevant. The fact is that the protagonist doesn't have to be even likeable. He has only to push the action forward. That's his job in the story, and that's the sole reason that he's identified as the protagonist.

A major cause for the confusion about the nature of the protagonist comes from Hollywood movies. Like television, commercial films have had a profound impact on contemporary cinematic storytelling. Rarely is the protagonist in a Hollywood movie an unlikable character. Usually, the character is more than simply appealing—he's too good to be true.

There are two very practical reasons for this. First, a great deal of money goes into a commercial Hollywood film—hundreds of millions of dollars—so studios don't want to risk driving away audiences by building a film around a character that is even faintly disagreeable. Second, the actors who play the leading roles are movie stars. At some point in their rise to stardom, their focus shifts from craft to fame and fortune. Because they are in the business of being stars (and because they are well compensated for it), they are reluctant to risk alienating their fans and undermining their star power, which a dark or unpleasant role could conceivably do.

But Hollywood's concerns shouldn't be your concerns, especially when you're creating a character. First and foremost, your protagonist needs to propel the action of the story. Beyond that, how the character is depicted is entirely up to you.

Sometimes, two or more characters share the responsibilities of the protagonist. In *Romeo and Juliet*, Romeo wants to keep his love with Juliet alive. She has a similar objective: to keep her love with him alive. He's not standing in the way of her objective, and she's not standing in the way of his. On the contrary, they are working together toward a common goal, their mutual love, and neither character is more important than the other in this pursuit. (The title is, after all, *Romeo and Juliet.*) When two or more characters act in this way, they are considered a **plural protagonist**.

Buzz Word

Plural protagonist: Two or more characters working together in pursuit of the same objective throughout the plot.

For a story to have a plural protagonist, three conditions must be met. First, the characters must share the same objective. Second, they must pursue that objective equally and cooperatively. Third, they must be teamed together throughout the course of the action.

Plural protagonists regularly appear in Hollywood **buddy movies**, and they are perhaps best known in this context. But they also appear in short films. When that happens, seldom do more than two characters function as the plural protagonist. As with many other aspects of the short film, there's simply not enough screen time for any more than that.

Like many protagonists, each of the characters making up the plural protagonist also has a need, which is typically the friendship, the love, or the assistance of the other character(s) who comprise the plural protagonist.

Buzz Word

Buddy movie: A film genre in which two friends (existing or soon-to-be) come together for the benefit of either or both.

Providing the main opposition to the protagonist, plural or otherwise, is the antagonist. Just as audiences are conditioned to think of the protagonist as a hero, so too do they tend to regard the antagonist as a villain. But an antagonist isn't inherently evil just as a protagonist isn't inherently good. Again, the character is defined by the specific dramatic function served. The protagonist propels the action, while the antagonist creates obstacles that complicate it. Both functions, propelling the action and creating obstacles, are the direct result of the characters' respective objectives.

When the protagonist and the antagonist have objectives that are diametrically opposed, they are locked in a **unity of opposites**: they are united in their opposition to each other. A unity of opposites occurs only when the objectives of the protagonist and the antagonist are irreconcilable. For example, if one character wants to kill another character and the second character is determined to live, a unity of opposites exists. The second character will either die or survive in some way. Those are the only two options, and there's no room for compromise.

In a short screenplay, creating a unity of opposites is especially desirable because it focuses the conflict, which then clarifies the action and heightens the dramatic tension. This is an unmistakable advantage when you have a limited amount of screen time to tell a story.

Buzz Word

Unity of opposites: A conflict in which a protagonist and an antagonist have objectives that are diametrically opposed.

The key to constructing a focused, dynamic conflict is creating an antagonist that is compelling to the audience in his own right. Whenever possible, he should have an objective, a need, an outlook, an attitude, and an arc.

The antagonist should also be a worthy opponent, equal in strength to the protagonist. The importance of this can't be overstated. If the protagonist is noticeably stronger than the antagonist—or vice versa—the outcome of the story is predetermined even before the film fades in. The stronger of the two will prevail, so there's no reason for the audience to bother watching.

It's important to keep in mind that strength—the possession and use of it—is specific to the conflict at the center of the plot. If, for instance, an industrial tycoon and his secretary are involved in a romantic relationship, they are equal in strength, despite the very different positions that they hold in society. This is so because their lives outside the main conflict, whether running board meetings or doing data input, are less important to the plot than their roles within the relationship.

Sometimes, two or more characters oppose the protagonist as a **plural antagonist**. Like a plural protagonist, the plural antagonist consists of characters that share the same objective. Unlike a plural protagonist, these characters don't necessarily work cooperatively. In fact, they may not even know each other if each is just one in a series of obstacles that the protagonist faces. Yet, whether they work together or serially, each of the characters must be of equal importance in the pursuit of the plural antagonist's objective.

Buzz Word

Plural antagonist: Two or more characters functioning as a single antagonist.

In Focus: Protagonist and Antagonist

A masked man bursts into an emergency room on the tough side of town and brandishes a gun with the intent to start shooting. A mild-mannered ER nurse overcomes her fear and in a rush of adrenalin disarms the intruder.

As people go, the nurse is essentially good and the intruder is essentially bad. But because the intruder is the driving force, the character pushing the action forward, he's the protagonist. Because the nurse intends to keep him from realizing his objective of harming the people awaiting treatment, she's the antagonist.

Why can't you reverse these functions? Why can't you argue that the nurse is just as much an agent for change and that she is in fact the protagonist, trying to keep her patients safe?

Here's why. If the intruder never enters the emergency room, there's no story. Life in the ER continues as it ordinarily would. If the nurse never tries to stop the intruder, there is a story but a much different and more unfortunate one. This makes the intruder the protagonist and the nurse the antagonist.

Secondary Characters

Often, a protagonist and an antagonist, even fully developed, aren't able to supply all the necessary action demanded by the plot or to communicate all the necessary information required by the story. In situations like these, two kinds of secondary characters are invaluable additions to your cast.

The **catalyst** is a character that causes something, usually just one thing, to happen. Protagonists and antagonists, by the very fact that they are pursuing objectives, make choices and cause things to happen. But they also do a great many other things. A catalyst is distinguished by a singularity of purpose. Causing something to happen is all he does. This type of character can be very useful when outlook or attitude or simple logistics prohibits your main characters from performing an action necessitated by the plot.

Buzz Word

Catalyst: A character whose sole purpose is to cause something to happen.

Another important type of secondary character is the **confidant**. The presence of a confidant allows another character, often the protagonist, to reveal himself by speaking his mind or disclosing his inner feelings.

Filmmaking is the art of making the internal external. Filmmakers attempt to do this through images and action. But the fact is that some ideas simply don't lend themselves to visual communication. A character just has to come right out and say what he's thinking or feeling.

Buzz Word

Confidant: A character whose sole purpose is to allow another character to reveal himself by speaking his mind and externalizing his feelings.

Certainly, you can have a character communicate information through **voiceover**, although the use of this device is sometimes regarded as lazy storytelling. (You should be able to dramatize every element of your story—or so the reasoning goes.) A character can also speak directly to the camera, although this device is extremely stylized, calling an undue amount of attention to itself. The more natural way to present information is through dialogue between two characters, one of which is a confidant.

Buzz Word

Voiceover: Narration, usually added in post-production, that occurs outside the immediate on-screen world of the film.

Perhaps you've noticed that the main characters in Hollywood movies always seem to have "buddies." These close friends exist chiefly to listen. Invariably, if a major character and a minor character are at a bar or in a restaurant or anyplace where people sit and talk, the minor character is acting as a confidant.

In using a catalyst or a confidant, you should always strive to make the character something more than a device, although that's clearly what he is. There's a reason that those movie buddies tend to be quirky or funny characters. The audience focuses on the quirkiness or the humor rather than the fact that important information is conveyed. What occurs, then, is a kind of dramatic sleight of hand, an instance in which characterization rather than character can make a difference.

Often in short films, one character may function as both a confidant and a catalyst. This provides the character with more of an on-screen presence by making him of greater importance to the story. Not incidentally, it also helps to limit the size of the cast.

In Focus: Catalyst

In a story that pits a detective against a wrongly accused murder suspect, some-one other than the suspect or the detective needs to have committed the murder, and so a catalyst is an absolute necessity. In this example, the catalyst sets the entire central action into motion because without a murder there would be no investigation and therefore no story.

An audience may connect with a film through its characters, but it will stay interested because of the plot. The reality is that even a character-centered screenplay is ultimately story-driven. Once you have established your characters in your mind and you know what they are capable of, it's time to put them to work. For that, you need a fuller understanding of the way a short screenplay is structured.

Chapter Two, Take Two—Chapter Review

- An audience makes its connection with a film primarily through identification with an empathetic character.
- In a short film, character is especially important because of the narrative and technical limitations inherent in the form.
- Characterization is the sum of all observable traits and qualities, which can be social, psychological, or physical in nature.
- The true nature of a character is defined by the choices that he makes and the actions that he takes during the course of the screenplay.
- There are five aspects of character:
    - Objective
    - Need
    - Outlook
    - Attitude
    - Arc

- There are four main types of characters:
  - Protagonist
  - Antagonist
  - Catalyst
  - Confidant
- A unity of opposites is a dramatic situation in which the protagonist and the antagonist have objectives that are diametrically opposed and irreconcilable.
- A plural protagonist consists of two or more characters pursuing a single objective equally and cooperatively and so acting together as a single protagonist.
- A plural antagonist consists of two or more characters pursuing a single objective in opposition to the protagonist.

Chapter Three

Narrative

"The challenge of screenwriting is to say much in little and then take half of that little out and still preserve an effect of leisure and natural movement."

Raymond Chandler, novelist, screenwriter

Key Concepts

- The five forms of conflict
- Setup, rising action, and resolution: the three-part nature of screenplay structure
- The importance of cause and effect
- Scene structure

Film is a medium of events. Important events. Dramatic events. Organizing these events in a meaningful and satisfying way is the most important task that you as a screenwriter take on.

The nature of traditional film narrative is such that events escalate in their intensity as the dramatic action progresses. What contributes to the escalation are obstacles that arise as the protagonist pursues his objective. Whenever a character encounters an obstacle, this meeting is called a crisis. A short-short will have one crisis; a long short will have many.

Any crisis is the direct result of the story's main conflict: the fundamental opposition between characters or between a character and a dramatic force. The main conflict takes one of five forms.

Character vs. Character

This is the commonest form of conflict and the simplest to establish. Your two main characters, the protagonist and the antagonist, are physically present in the plot and clearly connected in their opposition to each other.

Character vs. Self

Also known as internal conflict, this form of conflict arises when a protagonist has an objective and a need that are in opposition to each other. Logically, if there's an inner conflict, there must be an inner action. Film, though, is an external medium. So about an internal conflict, a screenwriter always has to ask, "How will I externalize it? What will the audience actually see of it on the screen?" A character can't simply walk around, mulling his fate, which is neither visual nor dramatic. Typically, another character is used to externalize the conflict in some way. As you can probably guess, this then tilts the conflict toward one of character versus character, blurring somewhat the original idea of an internal conflict.

Character vs. Society

In this form of conflict, society is defined as an established authority of any kind: government (including the military and intelligence services), church, school administration, etc. It may even be a less bureaucratic organization like a sorority or a scout troop.

Depicting this form of conflict raises a practical question: how does the screenwriter embody "society"? A character can't literally take on an entire government or a branch of the military. There's simply no effective way to dramatize something so expansive. For this reason, society is frequently represented by a character that's the leader or the opinion-maker for the group depicted in the story. Here again, a seemingly distinct form of conflict can resemble that of character versus character.

Character vs. Nature

Conflicts with nature occur in one of two ways: externally or internally. External conflicts with nature involve living things (a great white shark, a whale, a tiger), natural occurrences (a twister, a hurricane, a tsunami, a landslide, an avalanche), or geography (a mountain to be climbed, a sea to be sailed, a desert to be crossed). Internal conflicts with nature involve natural processes of a more personal kind: ageing or illness, for example.

Character vs. Fate

This form of conflict is seldom seen in film, although it was often found in ancient Greek theater at a time when defying the gods held the promise of disastrous consequences. Today, people rarely believe in fate to the degree that tempting it would be a serious focus of a conflict.

The Three-Part Nature of the Screenplay

Smart Quote

"Life is dramatic, but its drama cannot be defined and presented without departures from life's usual procedures."

Eric Bentley, literary critic

Action flows directly from conflict. Whether a film is short or long, its action is structured in three parts: setup, rising action, and resolution. These correspond roughly to the beginning, the middle, and the end of a story—any story. Although the goals and the focus of each part differ, they share one thing in common: a need for conciseness. A short film should be, after all, short.

The setup is the first of the three parts. As the term suggests, it's the portion of the film that sets up key elements:

Setting

The setting is the time and the place of the action—for example, Oklahoma during the Great Depression or New York City today.

Backdrop

The backdrop provides a specific milieu in which the story takes place. This might be tied to a location (a racetrack, a boarding school, a hospital), or it might be linked to a line of work or a way of life (a police department, the ministry, or a theater troupe).

Tone

The tone reflects the general sensibility of the film—light or brooding, ironic or sincere, subtle or over the top, and so forth.

Protagonist

A short film is finally the story of its protagonist, so that character should always be introduced as early as possible in the action.

A hint of the conflict to come

Just as there's not enough time for a complete, 180-degree transformation of a character in a short film, so too is there not time enough to develop a conflict when absolutely none exists. Inherent in the characters, their relationship, or their world must be something that will allow a conflict to surface rapidly and convincingly. In other words, the conflict should begin to take shape even before fade-in.

The direction of the plot

The setup should contain at least a suggestion of the direction in which the action is headed. Of course, this doesn't mean divulging the entire plot. What would be the point of writing the rest of the screenplay? It does mean laying the groundwork for what's to come. If you're telling a story about a woman who's looking for her long lost husband, for example, the audience should understand that the central action of the story is going to involve a search.

The inciting incident

The inciting incident is the event that sets the action into full motion. In a feature-length screenplay of 100–120 pages, it usually takes place in the first ten or so pages, which is in the middle of the setup. In a short screenplay, it usually occurs at the end of the setup where the **rising action** is launched.

Buzz Word

Rising action: The plot's main structural part, consisting of a variety of escalating struggles that culminate in the climax.

The setup of your screenplay should contain all these elements. If it doesn't, you should make the necessary changes to ensure that it does.

Your goal is always to set up your plot as quickly as possible. Much has been written about feature-length screenplays and their three-act structure in which the setup and resolution are approximately the same length (20–30 pages) and the rising action is about twice as long as either (45–60 pages). But short screenplays, as you know, aren't simply briefer versions of feature-length screenplays.

In a short-short of two to four pages, there's almost no time at all for the setup. At most, it should be completed by the middle of the first page of the screenplay. In a conventional short of seven to twelve pages, it should be completed no later than the middle of the second page. A medium short of 20–25 pages provides the screenwriter with slightly more time, but the setup should still be completed in the first three to five pages. A long short will have a setup of five to ten pages, depending on the overall length of the screenplay: a 30-page screenplay will have a setup of no more than five pages, a 60-page screenplay no more than ten.

Keep in mind that these page limits are only guidelines. Whenever possible, an even shorter setup is preferable. If, for example, you're writing a 45-page screenplay and the setup is complete by the third page, you're ahead of your audience and well on your way to developing a briskly paced film.

Screenwriter's Notebook: How Long Should the Setup Be?

Screenplay	Setup
Short-short (2–4 pages)	No more than one-half page
Conventional short (7–12 pages)	1–$1/2$ pages
Medium short (20–25 pages)	3–5 pages
Long short (30 or more pages)	5–10 pages, depending on the overall length of the screenplay

One of the challenges in writing the setup is that certain information important to the understanding of the plot isn't clear from the events on-screen. **Exposition** is the device that provides this information, which usually pertains to an existing relationship between characters (childhood sweethearts, sworn enemies, half-brothers) or a situation (a recent divorce, the anniversary of a death, a forgotten birthday). Most often, exposition is handled through dialogue, although newspaper headlines, television and radio broadcasts, and street signs have all been used at one time or another.

Buzz Word

Exposition: A narrative device providing information not evident from the events on the screen but necessary to the audience's understanding of the plot.

The main problem with exposition is that, generally, it exists only for the benefit of the audience. The characters are already aware of the information because it's a part of their world. Exposition, then, is motivated not by an event intrinsic to the story but by the audience's need to know. When handled badly, exposition comes off as stilted and obvious. When handled skillfully, it's evidence of a screenwriter with a great deal of craft.

Exposition should not be confused with **back-story**, which consists of events in the lives of the characters prior to fade-in. Back-story is information, while exposition is a device. Typically, some very small part of the back-story is revealed through exposition, but the most important facts come out through **revelation**.

Buzz Word

Back-story: Significant events in the lives of the characters occurring prior to fade-in and affecting the action as it unfolds. Also written as *back story* or *backstory*.

Revelation: The dramatic disclosure of information that furthers the plot.

Unlike exposition, which provides the audience with an understanding of the context of the action, revelation is a dramatic device, pushing the action forward. Because exposition is narrative rather than dramatic in nature, it should be used only in the earliest moments of the setup. Revelation can be used at any point in the action up to and including the resolution.

Rising Action

Once the rising action is set into motion, the central conflict—also known as the problem of the story—emerges. As with most problems, someone tries to find a solution. In this case, the protagonist develops a plan. Simply by doing what he does in the course of the action, the protagonist will be indicating the plan that he has developed—that is, he doesn't actually have to come right out and explain his intentions.

The gap between the protagonist's expectations for the plan and the reality of what actually happens forms the basis for the developing action, which consists of a series of struggles, prompted by a crisis or crises. These crises cause the protagonist to make choices and to take action even as he continues to pursue his objective. Meanwhile, the crises escalate in intensity, each greater than the one preceding, as the action nears its climax.

Note

Remember that a crisis occurs whenever a character encounters an obstacle, which can be emotional, psychological, or physical.

Because the rising action comprises so much of the dramatic action, keeping your audience engaged is critical. Each crisis should appeal to the audience in one of three ways: concern for the characters, curiosity about the direction of the plot, or some combination of the two.

While the characters and the circumstances of each scene help to determine its appeal to an audience—emotional or intellectual or both—the way that dramatic information is conveyed also plays a part. A screenwriter must decide how much information the audience should know relative to the characters on-screen. When the audience knows less than the characters, there's naturally curiosity about the outcome of the events on-screen. This storytelling strategy is called **mystery**. When the audience shares the same information as the characters, there's both concern for the characters and curiosity about the outcome. This strategy is called **suspense**. When the audience knows more than the characters, there's only concern for the characters because the outcome is already known. This strategy is called **dramatic irony**.

Buzz Word

Mystery: A narrative strategy in which the audience knows less than the characters about what is taking place on-screen.

Suspense: A narrative strategy in which the audience possesses the same information as the characters about what is taking place on-screen.

Dramatic irony: A narrative strategy in which the audience knows more than the characters about what is taking place on-screen.

A screenplay may use more than one strategy. Each character is in possession of different information, and that can cause a shift in strategy from scene to scene as the cast of characters on-screen changes. Knowing when to use the appropriate strategy is an important screenwriting skill, and it's developed largely through experience over time.

Beyond these three storytelling strategies, keeping the audience engaged in the rising action sometimes requires incorporating more of the underlying story into the dramatic action. This is done through the addition of a B-plot.

This subplot provides a second line of action, increasing the variety and the number of events on-screen. Interwoven with the events of the A-plot, it may also reflect a different side of the protagonist, creating an opportunity to examine the character more fully.

A B-plot may be as elaborate as an A-plot with as many characters and crises, or it may be a relatively minor subplot, requiring only a few scenes and one or two characters. A long short generally has a B-plot. Often, a medium short does, too. But a B-plot should never appear in either a short-short or a conventional short because there's simply not enough screen time to accommodate it. In these briefer films, a subplot serves only to split the focus of the audience and undermine the impact of the main plot.

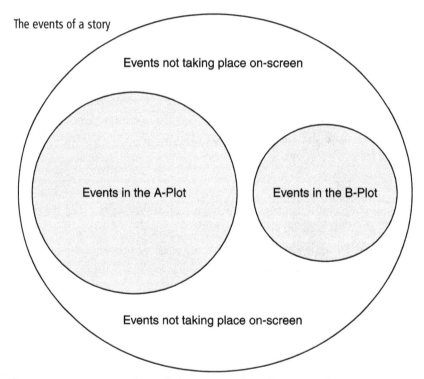

Figure 3.1 You may use the underlying events from the story in the A-plot, the B-plot, or not at all.

Whether or not there is a B-plot, scenes are linked throughout the action through **cause and effect**. What occurs in the first scene leads directly to what occurs in the second scene. What occurs in the second leads directly to what occurs in the third. And so on.

Buzz Word

Cause and effect: The principle that an action or an event will produce a response in the form of another action or event.

Without a clear cause and effect, there's a sense of randomness to the order and the intensity of scenes as well as a reliance on coincidence. When scenes don't connect through cause and effect, the structure is considered **episodic**. Because traditional film narrative favors plots that are linear and dynamic, an episodic structure should be avoided in screenplays of this kind.

Buzz Word

Episodic: Lacking a clear cause and effect between scenes or dramatic moments.

One device in particular, the plural antagonist, has the tendency to increase the likelihood of an episodic structure. This is because those characters that comprise the plural antagonist often work serially and independently of one another, so the obstacles set up by them may lack a clear dramatic connection to one another. This isn't to suggest that a plural antagonist should be avoided entirely. However, you should be aware of the potential pitfalls before using this device.

In Focus: Cause and Effect

In the first scene of "The Red Balloon," the young boy finds the red balloon in the street. In the second scene, he takes the balloon to a bus stop where he waits for a bus. In the third scene, the balloon and he encounter their first obstacle when they are stopped from boarding a city bus. Without the first scene in which he finds the balloon, the boy could not take it to the bus stop. Without the second scene in which he arrives at the bus stop, he could not attempt to board the bus. Clearly, each scene leads to the one that follows.

Some Additional Devices

Keeping the rising action rising is a challenge for every screenwriter. There's help, though. To increase dramatic tension, to maintain a sense of cause and effect, and to sustain audience interest, you have a number of devices at your disposal.

Condition lock

With a time lock, which you learned about earlier, you create a deadline for something to be done...or else. With a condition lock, you create a requirement that must be met for an objective to be realized or for a conflict to be resolved.

Typically, the requirement can be summarize in an if-then statement. If the teenage girl can't convince her parents that her boyfriend is Mr. Right, then they won't let her see him again. If the runner doesn't break a five-minute mile in the track meet, then he won't qualify for the athletic scholarship that will allow him to go to college. If the terrorists don't receive $5,000,000 in ransom, then they will kill the hostages one by one until they do.

A condition lock heightens dramatic tension in much the same way that a time lock does. It puts very clear limits on the characters and gives direction to the action.

Plant and payoff

Coincidence is the enemy of traditional film narrative, which requires the consistent and credible use of cause and effect. Planting involves subtly presenting information to an audience so that, when it's used to greater dramatic effect later in the action, it neither seems coincidental nor requires explanation.

In the opening scene of *The Godfather*, one of the wedding guests seeking a favor from Don Corleone happens to be an undertaker. He's the same undertaker who's later summoned to prepare the bullet-riddled body of Sonny Corleone for his funeral. When he receives Sonny's dead body at the funeral home in the middle of the night, no one in the audience wonders who he is or why the don would call on him specifically for this sensitive job. It's all been planted in the first scene of the film.

Planting and paying off is not the same thing as foreshadowing, which specifically hints at plot developments later to come. A good plant should barely draw the attention of an audience.

Red herring

To sustain interest, you never want an audience to get too confident about where the plot of your film is headed. A red herring is a device that misdirects or misleads the audience into making false assumptions about the characters or the plot.

In detective stories and thrillers, red herrings are often used to throw suspicion on characters that are otherwise innocent and to remove suspicion from the actual bad guys. Yet they can also be used in other, more inventive ways. In the film *Psycho*, the audience is led to believe that the mother of Norman Bates is a reclusive, foul-tempered old lady. It turns out that she's reclusive all right. But she's also dead.

While red herrings are regularly found in crime stories of every kind, they can be successfully used in films of any genre.

Climax

The rising action culminates in the climax, the point of greatest dramatic intensity in the screenplay. This usually occurs in an **obligatory scene**. Here, the major dramatic question is answered, and the conflict is resolved one way or another: the protagonist attains his objective or he doesn't. Either way, he'll make some sort of discovery about himself and understand the meaning of the struggle that he has just undergone.

Buzz Word

Obligatory scene: A scene implicitly promised to the audience through developments in the plot or the nature of the characters. The climax is almost always an obligatory scene because in film narrative a conflict demands a resolution.

Every climax shares certain characteristics. First, the protagonist is physically present for the scene. After all, the film is his story, so he should be on hand for its biggest moment. Second, the protagonist is connected to the moment. He has something at stake, and he knows it. Third, the scene is emotional and external, something that actors can play and that the audience can see and hear. So the climax is never an internal moment, even when it brings the resolution of an internal conflict.

Often, in a short film, the climax presents a twist, an unexpected plot turn that functions as a "surprise ending." In fact, the success of a short film is often judged by the cleverness and the appropriateness of this twist. Despite its popularity, a climax of this kind shouldn't be considered a necessity and, like novelty generally, it should never be pursued for its own sake. A twist should be the result of true surprise, surprise based in the authenticity of the characters, and not cheap surprise, an unexpected event that exists only to jolt the audience.

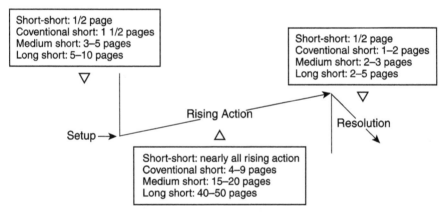

Figure 3.2 Page count and the three-part narrative structure.

With the climax comes the conclusion of the rising action. The length of the rising action, like the length of the setup, varies according to the overall length of the screenplay. Almost all of a short-short will be rising action with the climax coming almost at fade-out. The rising action in a conventional short is typically four to nine pages long. A medium short may have 15 to 20 pages of rising action. A long short may have as many as 40 or 50 pages.

In Focus: Surprise Ending

In the classic short film "Occurrence at Owl Creek Bridge," an accused Confederate spy escapes from his captors, a troop of Union soldiers, just as he is about to be hanged. The twist is that his escape turns out to be an elaborate fantasy, taking place entirely in his mind, and that he is ultimately hanged. The climax is not only unexpected but also wholly appropriate because the film raises the thematic question, "What goes through a person's mind at the moment of death?"

Resolution

Smart Quote

"It's been my experience that an audience will forgive you almost anything at the beginning of a picture but almost nothing at the end. If they're not satisfied with the end, nothing that led up to it is going to help."

Robert Towne, screenwriter, director

Any plot or character questions still left open in the climax are answered in the resolution. It's here that the world of the story is finally realigned and an equilibrium of a kind returns.

But the resolution shouldn't be just a "falling action" or a tying up of loose ends. It presents one last opportunity for the screenwriter to reveal something about the story, the characters, and their world. Ideally, the resolution should be as important to the story as the climax that precedes it.

On occasion, the climax and the resolution are one, taking place in a single moment. Although the reasons for this convergence vary from screenplay to screenplay, generally the climax brings such finality to the events on-screen that there's no dramatic point to continuing.

In "Occurrence at Owl Creek Bridge," the accused Confederate spy has been in conflict with faceless Union troops, a plural antagonist, throughout the action. Because the audience has no compelling interest in the troops once the protagonist is dead, there's no reason to go any further. The climax is in fact the end of the story.

When a conflict is resolved with this sort of finality and a plot is ended with this sort of conclusiveness, the resolution of the screenplay is considered a **closed ending**. Sometimes, though, the audience is brought to the climax of the story and asked to make its own judgment about the way everything will turn out. When the conflict is left partially or fully unresolved or the plot lacks a sense of finality, the resolution is considered an **open ending**. The danger in writing an open ending is that it can seem coy or evasive or just plain arbitrary. Open endings should be used judiciously and only for legitimate thematic or dramatic reasons.

Buzz Word

Closed ending: An ending that both resolves the conflict and brings a conclusive end to the plot.

Open ending: An ending that leaves the conflict partially or entirely unresolved and the plot without a definite conclusion.

In Focus: Open and Closed Endings

A verdict is about to be read in the climax of a courtroom drama. If the jury actually delivers its verdict and the audience sees the consequences of it, there's a closed ending. If, on the other hand, the film fades out just as the foreman says, "We, the jury find the defendant…," there's an open ending.

Scenes

A plot is really nothing more than a series of dramatically significant moments. The success of your screenplay rests not only on the selection and ordering of those moments but also on the way that each scene is structured to incorporate them. Scene construction is similar to plot construction in many ways, though there are important differences. Before examining the similarities and differences, you need to be absolutely clear on what a scene is.

A scene is the basic building block of the screenplay. It's a unit of dramatic action distinguished by *unity of time* and *proximity of space*. A single scene may take place in several locations as long as they are adjacent and the action is continuous. A long, dialogue-intensive scene (best avoided in a short screenplay) might begin with a husband and a wife talking in the kitchen, continue as they move through the living room, and then conclude as they arrive in the bedroom. One continuous action and three adjacent locations equal one scene.

Although the use of multiple locations in a single scene may answer any number of narrative or dramatic needs, it's often motivated by nothing more than visual interest. The audience wants to see something more than two heads talking. This type of dialogue-intensive scene in which characters move and talk is so common that it has a name: a walk-and-talk.

It's important to understand that, when a film is in production, the definition of a scene changes. Location rather dramatic action becomes the determining factor. In production, any change in location represents the beginning of a new scene. In other words, a scene that spans three locations in your screenplay will be considered three separate scenes when in production.

Although this distinction may seem confusing at first, it arises from two different but equally important concerns. The screenwriter is focused on story events and the way they come together to form a plot. The production team is focused on physical production, including scheduling and budgeting. More locations mean more time and more money.

What provides unity in any scene in a screenplay, whether it uses multiple locations or just one, is the main action at its center. Every scene is built around a single main action known as a **major beat** or a story event. In this action, a character or a dramatic force does something significant, which can be expressed in a single sentence: the lovers meet, Romeo takes the poison, Juliet discovers the body. While a great many things may happen during the course of a scene, its essence—its overriding storytelling purpose—remains a single action.

Buzz Word

Beat: A unit of action defined by the occurrence of a change. Beats can be divided into two categories: (1) *major beats* (also called story events) in which the change is so great that it moves the plot forward; (2) minor beats, which are the smaller changes that make up the underlying structure of any given scene.

With that single central action as a spine, a scene must accomplish one of three goals:

1. Advance the plot
2. Reveal character
3. Deepen the audience's understanding of the story by disclosing back-story, providing insight into the backdrop of the story, or conveying theme

An especially good scene accomplishes two of these goals. The most effective sort of scene accomplishes all three.

No matter how effective a scene is, though, it can't continue indefinitely. Once it no longer accomplishes at least one of these goals, it should end. And when the scene is over, something in the world of the story must be different—there must be a change.

Sometimes, a change is so great that it takes the plot in a completely different direction. This 180-degree change is called a **reversal**. Invariably, a reversal surprises the audience. However, you should make sure that your surprise is true rather than cheap.

Buzz Word

Reversal: A change so extreme that it causes the plot to reverse itself and go in an entirely different direction.

If, by the end of the scene, nothing has changed in the world of the story, it must be cut from the screenplay. No film can afford to include scenes that merely take up time or amuse the screenwriter. This is especially true for a short film.

Smart Quote

"Every little scene that you can cut, you cut."

William Goldman, screenwriter

Some scenes are not truly scenes at all—at least, not dramatic ones. A **bridge scene** provides a narrative link to a full, dramatic scene, but it has no dramatic purpose of its own.

A jet plane lands on a runway before a scene in an airport terminal. A crowd files into a football stadium before a scene set in a locker room. A man gets out of the car in his driveway and starts up the walkway before a scene set in the living room of the house. These are all examples of bridge scenes.

Buzz Word

Bridge scene: A brief scene that provides a transition into a dramatic scene but has no dramatic purpose of its own.

This sort of pseudo-scene is useful in establishing the facts of the real scene that follows: the time, the place, and any special circumstances. It also provides a way to "open up" a film that is largely set in interior locations.

Bridge scenes, though, should be used only when absolutely necessary. Scenes in which characters walk or ride from one location to another without any legitimate narrative purpose should be avoided. They slow the pace of the action, and they require additional setups and shots in production.

Scene-protagonist vs. Scene-antagonist

Along with a single main action, every scene also has a single protagonist propelling it. The **scene-protagonist** needn't be the screenplay's main protagonist. An antagonist, a catalyst, or even a confidant can serve this dramatic function. Whoever the scene-protagonist is, the **scene-objective** should reflect some aspect of that character's main objective or need. The term **super-objective** is often used to distinguish a character's main objective in the film from an objective specific to any particular scene.

Buzz Word

Scene-protagonist: The character whose scene-objective drives the action in any particular scene.

Scene-objective: The goal that motivates a character's actions and choices in a scene. It should reflect some aspect of the character's super-objective or need.

Super-objective: The goal that drives a character's choices and actions throughout the screenplay.

Scene-antagonist: The character that provides the main opposition to the scene-protagonist as that character pursues his scene-objective.

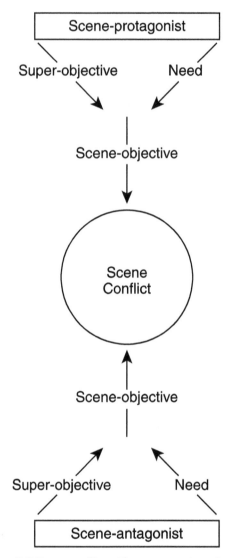

Figure 3.3 Scene conflict with a scene-antagonist present.

Usually, obstacles within a scene are created by the scene-antagonist, which can be any of the film's characters: protagonist, antagonist, catalyst, or confidant. Like the scene-protagonist, the scene-antagonist will have a scene-objective that reflects some aspect of either his super-objective or his need.

Sometimes, though, there's no scene-antagonist present in a scene. In this case, another dramatic force—self, nature, or society—provides an obstacle, which forms the basis for the scene-conflict. If, for example, a detective is searching a room for evidence of a crime, he's in conflict with nature, in this case the immediate environment of the room. The alignment of objects and furnishings in the room conceals potential evidence and so provides an obstacle that he must overcome to realize his scene-objective.

No matter how obstacles are created, whether by a scene-antagonist or by some other dramatic force, the structure of the scene is still a microcosm of the three-part structure of the screenplay. Each scene has a setup, a rising action, and a climax. The scene begins with a very brief setup followed by an inciting incident. That sets the rising action into motion, and a scene-conflict develops. The conflict pushes the rising action to its highest point, the climax of the scene. Instead of resolving the conflict completely like the main climax, this climax propels the action into the next scene.

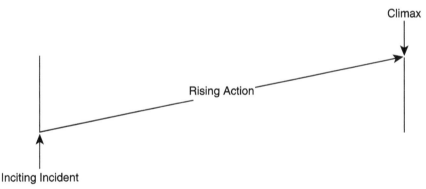

Figure 3.4 Scene structure.

The way that a scene builds is critical. The **point of attack** comes as late as possible, ideally with the central action of the scene in progress. In other words, the scene is not starting from a standstill. Things are already happening. The conflict then intensifies gradually and progressively in a series of minor beats. The most important beat is saved for the climax of the scene, so the scene has room to grow. To move that beat earlier in the scene would make everything coming after it anticlimactic, bringing the forward movement of the dramatic action to a temporary halt and leaving a dead spot in the film.

Point of attack: The point in the story at which a scene or the plot begins.

Unlike a major beat, which is a story event that moves the plot forward, a minor beat brings about incremental change. Anytime a character enters a scene, performs some significant physical action, or displays an adjustment in emotion or psychology, no matter how slight, a new beat occurs. Minor beats are the necessary connective moments between major beats. Without them, a scene would seem disjointed and unnatural. They turn plot into structure.

A two-page scene may have ten or more minor beats. A one-page scene may have half as many, although it should never have fewer than three, which would correspond to the setup, the rising action, and the climax.

A scene can be extraordinarily brief, no more than a paragraph in the screenplay, but it should never extend beyond three pages, preferably two. The reality is that even the cleverest cinematographer begins to run out of angles after that many pages, and an already long scene on paper will seem even longer on-screen as the camerawork begins to repeat itself.

If a scene runs long, you have two options: make internal cuts within the scene, pruning lines and beats, or divide the scene into two or more smaller scenes. If you opt for the latter, be sure that each of the new shorter scenes contains a major beat. If not, the correct strategy is to cut the scene internally. Today, the tendency among screenwriters, working on either short screenplays or long screenplays, is to write a greater number of briefer scenes.

Creating the Scene

Before you begin to write a scene, you must ask yourself a series of questions:

What is the dramatic point of the scene?

What are you trying to accomplish in the overall structure of the screenplay with the scene?

What is the major beat in the scene?

Identify the single main action that the scene will be built around.

Which characters do I need to make the scene work?

Using fewer characters is always better both for reasons of audience engagement and for the health of your production budget.

Who is the scene-protagonist?

This is often expressed by the question, "Whose scene is this?"

What does the scene-protagonist want in the scene?

What is the character's scene-objective? The protagonist of every scene has one.

What is the form of the conflict in the scene?

Is the conflict in the form of character versus character, character versus self, character versus society, or character versus nature? If the conflict is character versus character, who is the scene-antagonist and what is his scene-objective? If there is no scene-antagonist, what is the dramatic force opposing the scene-protagonist?

What is the subtext for the scene?

What is going on below the surface—the unspoken thoughts and concealed feelings that contribute to the scene's true meaning?

Where will the scene play?

The choice of a location for a scene is very often arbitrary. An idea pops into the screenwriter's head, the location seems natural enough, and so that's the way it stays. Yet, the fact is that the vast majority of scenes are not inextricably tied to the location where they take place. And a particular location, while certainly credible, may not be visually interesting. This can be a missed opportunity because film is a medium whose great power lies in images, and an arresting or unusual location can add a visual context that would not otherwise be present in a scene.

At what time of day will the scene play?

Scenes shot at night can be dramatically and visually effective. But to capture *any* image at night requires more lighting equipment and a larger crew than shooting during the day. To capture a truly interesting image requires even more lighting equipment and an even larger crew. Also keep in mind that scenes set specifically at sunrise and sunset will be virtually impossible to shoot at precisely those times of day. Sunrise will turn into day very rapidly as will sunset into night. The best advice is to set a scene during the day, unless there is a clear and compelling dramatic purpose for setting it at night.

Once you have answered these questions, you can begin laying out the scene, determining the way the action will unfold and outlining the minor beats. And once you know what the characters will do in the scene, you can finally begin to concern yourself with what they will say. While understanding the principles of film dialogue is critical for any screenwriter, it's especially so for someone writing a short film.

Chapter Three, Take Two—Chapter Review

- There are five forms of conflict:
    - Character vs. character
    - Character vs. self
    - Character vs. nature
    - Character vs. society
    - Character vs. fate
- Traditional narrative screenplays are structured in three parts:
    - Setup
    - Rising action
    - Resolution
- As the term setup suggests, the first part of the screenplay sets up key elements:
    - Setting
    - Backdrop
    - Tone
    - Protagonist
    - A hint of the conflict to come
    - The general direction of the plot
    - The inciting incident

- In the rising action, the protagonist faces a series of struggles that escalate in intensity as they near the climax, the highest dramatic point in the action.

- Any plot or character questions still left open in the climax are answered in the resolution. It's here that the world of the story is finally realigned and equilibrium is restored.

- In an open ending, the conflict is partially or entirely unresolved, and the plot is left without a definite conclusion.

- In a closed ending, the conflict is fully resolved and the plot is brought to a conclusive end.

- Scenes are linked throughout the screenplay by cause and effect, the principle that an action or an event will produce a response in the form of another action or event.

- The point of attack should come as late as possible, ideally with the central action for the scene already in progress.

- A scene can be extraordinarily brief, but it should never extend beyond three pages, preferably two, when visual interest becomes harder to maintain.

Chapter Four

Dialogue

"Uttering a word is like striking a note on the keyboard of the imagination."

Ludwig Wittgenstein, philosopher

Key Concepts

- The goals of film dialogue
- The characteristics of film dialogue
- Structuring scenes and speeches
- Making every line count

Just as characters aren't people, dialogue isn't conversation. Eavesdrop on someone, and you quickly realize that everyday conversation is rambling, repetitious, and remarkably inarticulate with gestures and body language often used to complete sentences and fill in thoughts. The fact is that two people can carry on a fairly lengthy conversation and say absolutely nothing of consequence. Talk, as the saying goes, is cheap.

In contrast, dialogue is dramatic speech. While it means to create an illusion of conversation, it eliminates all the excess baggage of conversation. It has a definite set of goals and a limited amount of time in which to achieve them.

Smart Quote

"Although I'll yield to no one in my reverence for movies as a visual art, they are not an entirely visual art. Dialogue gives tremendous resonance to movies."

Jay Cocks, screenwriter, film critic

The Goals of Film Dialogue

Film dialogue is a nonrenewable resource. Use it wisely and sparingly. Make sure that, in any line that you write, you accomplish at least one of six goals:

Move the plot forward.

Even in the most visual of screenplays, there may be some information that can't be expressed through images. Often, this information, communicated through dialogue, is important enough to further the plot.

Reveal character.

Dialogue can add depth to characters in two significant ways. First, a character can disclose important information about himself or his situation (although simple exposition, as you recall, should be limited to the setup of the screenplay). Second, the way a character speaks can reveal almost as much as the information that he is communicating. A classics scholar, for example, won't use the same vocabulary or the same grammar as a bricklayer.

Provide story information.

Beyond the basic information communicated through exposition, facts affecting the direction of the story may need to be disclosed through dialogue. Most aspects of the back-story will be revealed in this way. Off-screen developments may be revealed in this way too, although any truly significant off-screen event should be presented as an on-screen event.

Establish tone.

While the visual elements of a film will go a long way toward establishing tone, especially in a darker or more serious work, dialogue also contributes. In a comedy, for instance, characters should deliver lines that are funny. After all, laughter is what the film is going for. The dialogue in a more serious film, on the other hand, shouldn't be peppered with one-liners. You'll only end up confusing, rather than amusing, the audience.

Convey theme.

Theme, as you know, is the ultimate meaning of a film. Sometimes, dialogue is used to reinforce this meaning by providing a context for on-screen events. In a sense, the screenwriter is guiding the reaction of the audience to those events through the words that the characters speak. At other times, a character may actually come right out and state the film's theme, although in a subtle, natural way.

In Robert Towne's screenplay for the film *Chinatown*, the character Noah Cross warns, "You may think you know what you're dealing with—but, believe me, you don't." A misguided sense of confidence in one's perceptions is the film's main theme: we don't know what we don't know.

Naturally, you should be careful not to use dialogue to put too fine a point on your theme. For example, you don't want your characters saying something like "All's well that ends well" or "I guess the good really do die young."

Add to the backdrop of the story.

Because a backdrop is a specific social environment, there may be patterns of speech, not to mention behavior, particular to it. Typically, different occupations have their own jargon. Some of it is technical in nature; some is simply slang. Different parts of the country also have their own patterns of speech, as do some cities and neighborhoods.

Dialogue has to reflect the subculture of its characters. At the same time, authenticity shouldn't come at the expense of clarity. The audience needs to understand what the characters are saying, so you as the screenwriter must walk the line between being faithful to a particular style of speech and being clear to the audience.

To be effective, a line of dialogue must accomplish *at least* one of these six goals. If it doesn't, cut it. There's no room for wasted words in any film, especially a short one.

The Characteristics of Film Dialogue

All dialogue, be it in film or television or theater, shares certain superficial similarities. Writers write it, and actors act it. Beyond that, the differences in both style and substance are many.

In theater, dialogue often succeeds through the brilliance of its language and the complexity of the emotions and the ideas contained in that language. In a certain way, plays are about language, its emotional and intellectual possibilities and limitations.

Consider these examples of stage dialogue:

> "The truth is rarely pure and never simple. Modern life would be very tedious if it were either, and modern literature a complete impossibility."

> —Delivered by Algernon in *The Importance of Being Earnest* by Oscar Wilde

> "It's not the voting that's democracy. It's the counting."

> —Delivered by Dotty in *Jumpers* by Tom Stoppard

Lines like these succeed not only because of their considerable wit but also because theater is an aural experience. The audience comes to listen. In a play, the dramatic action is advanced directly through dialogue or through the consequences of that dialogue. Language can be as expansive or poetic as the playwright would like it to be just as long as it's consistently so.

Like theater, television uses dialogue to propel dramatic action. But because television dialogue is performed for a camera, which provides a high level of intimacy, language tends to be less heightened than dialogue written for the stage. From Jerry Seinfeld's famous entrée "What's the deal with…?" to Jackie Gleason's trademark "How sweet it is," the words are simple and direct.

In a sense, television dialogue has the worst of both worlds. It does the heavy lifting of driving dramatic action, but it's limited by the literalness of the medium. For comedy writers, writing dialogue is even tougher. Their words are constrained by the genre's formulaic rhythm of straight lines and laugh lines. Although many shows from *The Simpsons* to *Entourage* are getting away from traditional sitcom dialogue, a significant number of comedies still feature dialogue written in a familiar pattern: straight line, straight line, joke; straight line, straight line, joke; straight line, straight line, joke; and so on.

Unlike dialogue written for television or theater, dialogue written for film is generally a complement, existing to fill in the blanks left by the visual elements of the screenplay. It tends to be spare, helping to move each scene forward in a dynamic fashion.

Are there exceptions? Without a doubt. But for every screenwriter like Quentin Tarrantino, whose screenplays are largely about cultural references and previously seen films, there are hundreds more who write dialogue with compression and precision. The reality is that a short film that is all dialogue is a short film that will receive little attention.

Writing Effective Dialogue

To write effective dialogue for your screenplay, you need to understand the story that you're trying to tell as well as the plot that you'll derive from it. Without this knowledge, you can't reasonably expect dialogue to move the plot forward or to provide information about the story, two of its main functions. You must also imagine each of your major characters fully: objective, need, outlook, attitude, and arc. Otherwise, you'll have no way of knowing what your characters are capable of saying.

Note

Remember that there is a clear distinction between story and plot.

Only when your plot and your characters are absolutely clear to you should you begin to write the dialogue for your screenplay. When you do, keep in mind the following principles:

Write dialogue that's dynamic and progressive.

The meandering, repetitive, and incomplete nature of everyday speech is best left to everyday speech. Each line of dialogue represents a step in the overall design of your screenplay's structure. Be sure that each step moves the dramatic action forward.

Be concise.

Logically, the more dialogue you write, the less effective any single line will be. Choose your words carefully, and limit the number of lines of dialogue to the fewest needed to convey your intended meaning. The aim in writing dialogue is always to create the maximum impact with the minimum number of words.

Keep lines simple.

Dialogue needs to be understood by the audience the first time around. Don't write sentences so convoluted that the audience can't follow them and the actors can't speak them. Sentences that run on with many clauses are more appropriate for reading than speaking. At the same time, simple isn't simplistic. You shouldn't overstate ideas or emotions in the mistaken belief that the audience is a little too dull to understand your point.

Keep speeches short.

Monologues and soliloquies are best suited to the stage. If a character must make a speech in your screenplay, limit it to no more than three or four lines of dialogue. There's simply no way to make a long speech visually interesting and dramatically compelling. This is true no matter how well written the dialogue or how skilled the actor performing it.

A simple alternative to a long speech is a dialogue exchange. Take the lines that you would have presented in a speech and break them down into smaller parts spoken by two or more characters.

Take care in the way that you represent a dialect or an accent on the page.

Making dialogue come across as natural and lifelike often involves doing things like dropping the letter g from the ends of words (writin' instead of writing) or using non-standard words like "ain't" and "aight." Still, you should never spell dialogue in dialect phonetically in your screenplay. ("Yah, suh, ahm a-gonna set myself he-ah foy a spell and write me a movin' pitchah.") This slows down the reading, and it can make your screenplay difficult to understand.

A better solution is to indicate the type of dialect or accent in the scene directions when you introduce a character for the first time—something like "Bridget speaks with a noticeable Irish brogue." Then, write the dialogue itself in more or less Standard English with an occasional word suggestive of the particular dialect or accent.

Also remember to go easy on vocabulary unique to a certain style of speech. While striving for authenticity, don't overreach. A little slang goes a long way.

Along with the dos of dialogue come some don'ts. Here are some things to stay clear of:

Don't turn every beat through the dialogue.

In other words, don't chart out every emotional change through what the characters say. Actors act, and they don't require pages of dialogue to do it. Instead, think visually. A look or a gesture or a physical action can move the scene forward as surely and emphatically as a line of dialogue.

Don't write "on the nose."

Like people, characters are not always forthcoming in their feelings or direct in their intentions. The real sense of a scene, then, isn't always apparent from the words that the characters speak. **Subtext** is the meaning underlying a character's actions and words. Because it occurs below the surface, a screenwriter creates layers of depth and a sense of reality through its use. Characters who speak their mind all the time are not especially believable. What's worse, in a very brief span of time, they can become inadvertently comical.

Buzz Word

Subtext: The underlying, unspoken meaning of a line of dialogue, a speech, or a scene.

Avoid filler phrases.

Phrases like "you know," "I mean," and "you hear me?" are best left out of dialogue. They take up valuable screen time without adding anything of importance to the characters or the plot.

Avoid stammering or stuttering except when the dramatic situation absolutely demands it.

Obviously, there may come a time in your screenplay when a character, out of fear or anxiety or despair, struggles to find the right words to say. That's natural. But you should never use stammering and stuttering simply to suggest naturalness of speech. Very often, the actors on the set supply the more naturalistic aspects of film dialogue, including stammering, stuttering, and other interruptions in the flow of speech. There's no reason to add more than they invent.

Don't be inflexible (unless you enjoy extreme frustration).

In filmmaking as in life, stuff happens. No matter how well crafted your screenplay is, the dialogue that you write will probably undergo some sort of transformation during the production process.

Sometimes, changes are necessitated by simple logistics. A particular piece of blocking, for example, may require an additional line of dialogue to cover it. At other times, dialogue may evolve as a part of the collaborative process. Film actors, unlike stage actors, sometimes shape their dialogue to accommodate their performance.

What this means is that a line that you have toiled over may be wiped away on the set with a single stroke of the script supervisor's pen. Whether this is right or wrong is irrelevant. It happens. Be prepared for it.

Screenwriter's Notebook: Visual Equivalents for Simple Expressions

Don't Say It	Show It
Yes Yeah Okay Sure	He nods
No Nah Nope	She shakes her head
Pleased to meet you How do you do?	They shake hands

Making Every Word Count

Smart Quote

"The most valuable of talents is never using two words when one will do."

Thomas Jefferson

Film dialogue—every last word of it—must have a purpose. It's no accident that the most memorable lines in film history seem curiously inconsequential when taken out of context:

"Go ahead—make my day."

"I'll make him an offer he can't refuse."

"Play it, Sam."

"Rosebud."

Film dialogue isn't an exercise in wit or wisdom, poetry or philosophy. It's inextricably tied to the here and now of the story being told.

Writing dialogue, perhaps more than writing any other element of the screenplay, requires enormous discipline. The compressed nature of film dialogue has a lot to do with it. But there's something else.

Every screenplay seems to have a line or two (or more!) that the screenwriter has fallen head-over-heels in love with. Very often, this infatuation is the only reason that these lines find their way into the script. To counteract this, every screenwriter is well advised to go over each completed scene with a very thick, very black pen and to cross out every one of his favorite lines. What will be left is dialogue that serves the screenplay, not the ego of the screenwriter. The best and most famous advice on this subject comes from the poet Keats. "First," he wrote, "kill all your darlings."

If an audience is thinking about the cleverness of the screenwriter, it's not focused on the film playing on the screen. The hand of the screenwriter should be invisible in the screenplay, just as the screenplay should be invisible in the completed film.

Once the deadwood of non-essential lines has been cleared away, a pattern develops in the dialogue. The brevity of the lines on the page gives exchanges between characters a staccato, back-and-forth quality—almost like a verbal Ping-Pong game.

In the following exchange, a wife returns home after a week out of town with suspicions that her husband, an ambitious lawyer, is having an affair.

> SUSAN
> How's Green versus the State of Illinois going?

> ANDERS
> Nightmare. I've never been so busy.

> SUSAN
> I tried to call you this week.

> ANDERS
> When?

> SUSAN
> A few times.

                         ANDERS
          I was at the office every night.

                          SUSAN
          That's where I called.

                         ANDERS
          I must have been in with one of the
          partners, I guess.

                          SUSAN
          I guess.

Because this scene involves suspicions that could threaten the characters'
marriage, the actors would play it deliberately without a trace of the staccato suggested by the words on the page. That's because actors act rather
than recite. The pacing of **line-readings** and the picking up of cues would
vary enormously throughout the scene. Pauses would be taken; looks would
be exchanged; blocking would be followed.

Buzz Word

Line-reading: The way a line of dialogue is performed by an actor.

By limiting dialogue to only the essential words, you create an uncluttered
cinematic space that gives an actor room to perform. It's a paradox of film
acting that having fewer lines to say often leads an actor to greater expres-
siveness and deeper meaning in a performance. As the actor Bonnie Bedelia
once explained, "I never let lines get in the way of my scene."

Naturally, some dialogue exchanges require more lines than others. Still,
even when characters speak two and three lines in a row, the back-and-
forth quality of the dialogue is never lost.

Smart Quote

"The right word may be effective, but no word was ever as effective as a rightly
timed pause."

Mark Twain

Because you are trying to approximate speech and because people speak largely in phrases, complete and grammatically correct sentences are neither necessary nor even particularly desirable in dialogue. Finding the fewest number of words capable of carrying the greatest weight—whatever the emotion or the idea expressed—is always the goal, even if the rules of grammar have to be tossed aside to do it.

Here's an example in an exchange between two teenage friends about to be separated by a family move.

```
                    ROBIN
          (writing on a scrap of paper)
     My new address.


                    ALIX
     Call me when you get there.


                    ROBIN
     If they have telephones.


                    ALIX
     Right.


                    ROBIN
     Later.
```

Just as important as the number of words is their order. In a line, a speech, or even an entire exchange, the most important point occurs at the end. The second-most important point occurs at the beginning. Everything else fills in the middle.

This is especially true for comedy. There's no surer way of killing a joke than to put the funniest part of it in the middle of a line or a speech. A punch line is always the last line. And the joke should become clear—and funny— only when the last word of that last line has been spoken.

In some languages, the verb is always placed at the end of the sentence. This forces a listener to remain attentive as the speaker withholds the most critical element of the sentence—the action taking place—until last.

Except in the simplest of sentences (he runs, she laughs, they pray), writers writing in English don't have this particular option of verb choice and placement. But, from those other languages, screenwriters can still take a lesson: save the best for last.

Keeping Dialogue Concise: A Case in Point

Early in the film *Full Body Massage*, Nina, an affluent art gallery owner, attempts to explain her life and career to the stranger who has unexpectedly appeared in her home. Here's the way that the speech read in an early draft of the screenplay:

```
                    NINA
I own a gallery. A few of them,
actually. One here in town, off
Melrose. One in New York, Tribeca.
Another in Chicago. They're very
successful, the three. They could be a
little more successful, of course. But
then I suppose you could say that
about anything, really.... It's a lot
of responsibility, though, having a
business like that—spread out across
the country. And when you're the one,
you know, when it's your business,
your baby—well, you know what they say
about responsibility falling on your
shoulders. It does—literally.
Mentally, emotionally, you feel it,
sure. But physically, too.
```

Although the dialogue seems natural enough with one line flowing into the next, the speech is simply too long for film. There's far too much talk and not nearly enough dramatic action to sustain it.

So how does the screenwriter go about cutting dialogue like this? The first question to ask is, what are the essential points that the character is trying to make? In this case, a close reading of Nina's speech reveals three: One, she has a successful art dealership. Two, maintaining the business can be challenging, sometimes a little too much. Three, the stress of her work is beginning to wear on her.

Keeping those three points in mind, the screenwriter began to cut anything that either failed to express at least one of these three points or, at the other extreme, repeated any of them:

```
                    NINA
      I own a gallery. A few of them,
      actually. One here in town, off
      Melrose. One in New York, Tribeca.
      Another in Chicago. They're very
      successful, the three. They could be a
      little more successful, of course. But
      then I suppose you could say that
      about anything, really.... It's a lot
      of responsibility, though, having a
      business like that — spread out across
      the country. And when you're the one,
      you know, when it's your business,
      your baby—well, you know what they say
      about responsibility falling on your
      shoulders. It does—literally.
      Mentally, emotionally, you feel it,
      sure. But physically, too.
```

With these cuts, there's a greater reliance on context and subtext to communicate essential information. Nina never comes right out and says that she's successful. The location of her galleries and their number do that for her. Similarly, the challenges of her work and its attendant stress, stated directly in the earlier version of the speech, are now left for the actor to play rather than say.

In the **production draft**, additional trimming and tweaking of the speech took place. Whether Nina owns two galleries or three galleries is less important than the fact that she owns more than one. So by giving her one fewer gallery to own, the screenwriter is able to cut even more dialogue.

Buzz Word

Production draft: The final draft of a screenplay written before a film goes into production.

When the scene went before the camera, the speech was one-third of its original size and looked like this:

                    NINA
    I own a gallery. A couple of them. One
    here in town, off Melrose. Another in
    New York, Tribeca. And when it's your
    business, your baby—well, you know
    what they say about responsibility
    falling on your shoulders. It does—
    literally.

In comparing the first version of the speech with the last, you can easily see that, despite the large number of cuts in dialogue, the meaning hasn't been lost. On the contrary, with all the excesses stripped away, its meaning is even clearer. Equally important, the shorter speech made for an easier scene for the actors to play and the crew to shoot.

While the cuts in this speech are extensive, most dialogue, regardless of its length, can usually benefit from some trimming. More often than not, this requires a scalpel rather than a chainsaw. But a skillful screenwriter, like an accomplished surgeon, should never be reluctant to cut whenever the patient requires it.

Character. Structure. Dialogue. These are the three major elements in cinematic storytelling. Yet, to begin writing a screenplay requires more than sitting down at a computer and typing the words, "FADE IN." Characters should be formed, a story designed, and the dramatic action plotted before a single word of the screenplay is written. All this is done through the process of development, which is the focus of the next chapter.

Chapter Four, Take Two—Chapter Review

- In the theater, the dramatic action is advanced directly through dialogue or through the consequences of that dialogue, and the language can be as expansive or poetic as the playwright would like it to be.

- In television, the dramatic action is advanced by dialogue, and the language tends to be literal and direct.

- In film, dialogue complements the visual elements of the screenplay and tends to be spare.

- Film dialogue has six goals:

  - Move the plot forward.

  - Reveal character.

  - Provide information about the story.

  - Establish tone.

  - Convey theme.

  - Add to the backdrop of the story.

- The dos of writing effective film dialogue:

  - Be concise.

  - Write dialogue that is dynamic and progressive.

  - Keep lines simple.

  - Keep speeches short.

  - Take care in the way that you represent a dialect or an accent on the page.

- The don'ts of writing effective film dialogue:

  - Don't turn every beat through dialogue.

  - Don't write "on the nose." Use subtext.

  - Avoid filler phrases.

  - Avoid stammering and stuttering except when the situation absolutely demands it.

  - Don't be inflexible. Dialogue often changes when a film goes into production.

- In a speech, a line, or an exchange, the most important point comes at the end, the second-most important point comes at the beginning, and everything else, which can vary in importance, lies in the middle.

Chapter Five

Development

"My movie is born first in my head, dies on paper; is resuscitated by the living persons and real objects I use, which are killed on film but, placed in a certain order and projected on to a screen, come to life again like flowers in water."

Robert Bresson, screenwriter, director

Key Concepts

- Generating ideas for your screenplay
- Developing your screenplay
- Writing your first draft
- Revising your screenplay

Having learned that the new guest at a party was a screenwriter, a woman with an interest in writing decided to approach him.

"I understand you're a screenwriter," she began. "I love to write. But I just don't know what to write about."

The screenwriter thought about it for a moment. Then, he shook his head and said, "Words are easy. Ideas are hard."

The party-going screenwriter may have overstated the ease of finding the right words to express himself, but he certainly didn't underestimate the difficulty of generating compelling ideas for film. The fact is, at any point in the creative process, coming up with the right idea is a challenge. At no time, though, is it more daunting than in the beginning, when you have nothing more than a blank page or a white computer screen in front of you.

Smart Quote

"Genius is one percent inspiration and ninety-nine percent perspiration."

Thomas Edison

Where Do Film Ideas Come From?

Unquestionably, many of the most memorable moments, lines, and plot developments in any film are the result of inspiration—that magical, inexplicable emergence of an idea seemingly out of the ether. But to do nothing until inspiration strikes you makes about as much sense as sitting around and waiting to win the lottery. As a screenwriter and a filmmaker, you can't leave your future to chance. You need to take matters into your own hands.

As a first step, think about the main story elements of a film: character, plot, setting (including backdrop), and theme. Each presents you with a way to begin to create your screenplay.

Character

Because short films are usually character-centered, using a specific character as a starting point makes a lot of sense. That character may be based on a person you know or someone you've heard about, or he may be a total invention. Of course, before a character can be of any real value to you, you must know what he wants *and* what he's willing to do to achieve it.

Plot

Plot presents you with several distinct ways to begin to create your screenplay. You can, for example, start with a **premise**. This might be something like the struggle of survivors in the aftermath of World War III or the relationship between an Afrikaner farmer and his servant during Apartheid or the tribulations of an aspiring actor whose car and possessions are stolen while on his way to California.

Buzz Word

Premise: The dramatic situation from which the conflict arises and the action unfolds.

By formulating a premise, you create a framework for the action of your screenplay and a context for your characters. But keep in mind that a framework and a context are all that you have. The next essential step is for you to identify a protagonist and to work out a central action.

Another possibility is to start with an inciting incident. This often takes the form of a "what if?" situation. For example, what if a man calls home from his car and, through a conversation with his four-year-old daughter, discovers that his wife is upstairs with another man? Or what if a desperately lonely woman encounters a man making a public appeal for romance on the Paris Metro?

Generally, if you know your inciting incident, you already have at least one of your characters in your head and perhaps even more. That's a good start. But you'll then need to answer two important questions. First, what happens after the inciting incident—that is, what are the main beats that make up the rising action? And, second, how does it all turn out—that is, what are the climax and resolution?

A third possibility is to come up with a central action, the overarching movement of the plot. In a short film, a central action may be as general as the breakup of a romance or the quest for revenge. It may be as simple as two strangers meeting on the street or a boy traveling through Paris with his red balloon. Devising a central action gives you an understanding of the overall direction of your plot. And because, broadly speaking, you know what's going to happen in your film, you have at least some sense of the characters you'll need to accomplish that.

Of course, you can have a clear idea for a central action and not know the climax and resolution. Just because you know what's going to happen in the setup and rising action doesn't mean that you know how the whole thing will turn out. If that's the case, your next step is to go straight to the end of your plot and come up with an appropriate climax and resolution.

A fourth possibility is to begin at the end—the climax. This is probably the most difficult way to approach an idea because it's rare that a screenwriter can devise a climax without having a sense of the plot that precedes it and the characters that cause it. Still, if a climax with a "twist" happens to pop into your head, you may find yourself starting at the end of the plot and working backward.

Setting

Sometimes a particular setting or backdrop will capture a screenwriter's imagination. Whether it's a place in time (Moscow at the end of the Cold War) or a social environment (sorority life) or a specific location (the bottom of the Grand Canyon), this kind of world can provide a vivid way for you to "see" your film. Unfortunately, only travel films are entirely about locations. In your short film, something must happen, and a character must cause that something to happen. So, if you start with a setting or a backdrop, your next step will be to identify a protagonist, a conflict, and a central action.

Theme

Perhaps, you're someone who is consumed by an important issue or a Big Idea. If that's the case, starting with a theme may be irresistible. It may in fact be the reason that you want to make films. Be careful, though. When you begin with a theme, you run the risk of writing a screenplay that's more like a treatise or an informational pamphlet. The characters may act less like recognizable individuals and more like mouthpieces for a particular point of view. Also keep in mind that, for many screenwriters, the theme of a film emerges only after writing several drafts of a screenplay. So, in starting with a theme, you may be putting the cart and the horse in something other than their customary order.

Screenwriter's Notebook: A Pathway for Creating Film Ideas

In a very real sense, every film is an experiment, and the creation of it is a journey into the unknown. Still, ideas for a screenplay can and often do evolve in a methodical way. The steps below show you a workable order for devising the various story elements of a screenplay. You can start with any step—even theme at the very bottom of the list. But if you start anywhere but the top, you should then go to Step 1 and make creating a premise the next element in your pathway. Once you've done that, follow the steps in order until you reach the bottom of the list.

Step 1   Premise

Step 2   Setting

Step 3   Protagonist

Step 4   Antagonist or opposing dramatic force

Step 5   Conflict

Step 6   Central action

Step 7   Inciting incident

Step 8   Climax and resolution

Step 9   Setup

Step 10   Rising action

Step 11   Theme

Development

Once you understand the story elements that you have to create, you need a way to pull them together. That's where development comes in.

In the world of commercial filmmaking, the word "development" conjures images of endless meetings with eager young executives dispensing extensive and often maddening script notes. But there's another, more positive sense of the term. Development can also be the process by which an idea for a film is broadened, refined, and improved through a thorough and deliberate effort on the part of the screenwriter.

"But wait," you may be saying. "Why do I have to develop anything? Why can't I just type 'Fade in' and begin writing?"

Two reasons: quality and speed. By totally familiarizing yourself with the underlying story of your screenplay and all its elements, you'll find that the writing process goes faster and that your creative output is more complete, more polished, and generally just better. The worst mistake that any screenwriter can make is to begin writing a first draft before completely understanding the material that it's based on. This leads to time wasted on writing lines, beats, and even entire scenes that will ultimately be cut from the script.

"But wait," you then may say. "I prefer to work intuitively, feeling my way through the creative process."

Here's the problem with that. Working by instinct is a lot like waiting for inspiration. When things are going well, they go very well. And when they are not, your writing comes to a grinding halt. Just as important, without a well-developed critical sense, without the ability to articulate what you're trying to accomplish dramatically and cinematically, you're at a disadvantage when problems arise in your screenplay and you need to find ways to fix them. You especially run the risk of changing things just for the sake of changing them rather than taking a more informed and constructive approach to revisions.

"But wait," you may persist. "Doesn't all this planning make for a contrived and artificial screenplay? Shouldn't everything just flow from my imagination directly onto the page to create a sense of authenticity?"

Well, no. Every film, even a documentary, is an invention. By its very nature, film is contrived and artificial. That's what a work of the imagination is.

The audience understands this and accepts it as long as there's consistency in the characters, the plot, and the world created on-screen.

Smart Quote

"When we experience a film, we consciously prime ourselves for illusion. Putting aside will and intellect, we make way for it in our imagination."

Ingmar Bergman, screenwriter, director

An audience will accept even impossible situations and worlds, provided that they are presented persuasively. Think of films like *Star Wars* and *Lord of the Rings*. Real? No. Even remotely possible? No. Credible? Yes. Audiences are drawn into these powerfully imagined worlds. Contrast that with a film that's "based on true story." The events, though real, might seem so far-fetched that the audience groans and giggles. "But," the screenwriter protests, "it really happened that way." The audience couldn't care less. As a screenwriter, you've got to earn the interest and respect of the audience. Remember Aristotle's famous words: "A convincing impossibility is preferable to an unconvincing possibility."

The Stages of Development

From concept to shooting script, screenplays are constantly in a state of evolution, and the development process reflects this. At different points in the process, you're developing different aspects of the screenplay. In the early stages of development, your concern is with the raw material of the story, including the main characters and the back-story. In the middle stages, the focus is on plot and structure. Then, the first and second drafts require combining all the elements in a coherent and dramatically satisfying way. By the time you've begun the production draft, your attention is exclusively on getting your screenplay ready for the camera.

Premise

Early in the development process, you need to establish the premise of your screenplay. The premise may be something that you write down, or it may just be something that you carry around in your head. But you need to know it, and you need to be able to express it clearly and succinctly, if only to yourself.

Because a premise is basically a situation, it's unchanging and not dynamic. It can tell you where you are, but it can't tell you where you're going. For that, you need a concept.

Concept

A concept is the idea for a story (not a plot) expressed in a single sentence. It consists of one sentence—and only one sentence—because you're looking for the essence of your story. In that single sentence, you identify the protagonist, that character's super-objective, and the main obstacle that stands in the way of the objective. Be sure to give some thought to the way you present your protagonist in your concept. Although an elaborate description isn't appropriate, you should try to include something more than just the character's name.

A concept is predictive, opening the possibilities of the story to you, the screenwriter. It's also something that you can refer back to as a sort of compass in the development process. However, don't confuse it with a **logline**, which is descriptive and usually created for the benefit of someone other than the screenwriter. Loglines are typically used for script submissions at studios, production companies, and talent and literary agencies. They are meant as memory joggers or talking points for executives rather than creative tools for screenwriters.

Buzz Word

Logline: A one- or two-sentence summary of the plot of a screenplay.

In Focus: Concept

Here are concepts for three especially effective short films:

- A boy and the very unusual balloon that he finds defy scorn, punishment, even violence to keep their friendship alive. ("The Red Balloon")

- A down-at-the-heels motorcyclist searches the streets and tunnels of London to turn a chance street encounter with a beautiful woman into the hookup of his dreams. ("Tunnel of Love")

- A renowned painter will lie, cheat, and even humiliate himself in order to hold onto the younger woman he loves—or at least thinks he does. ("Life Lessons" segment of *New York Stories*)

Title

A title isn't truly a separate stage in the development process, but it's worth serious mention at this point. Like a concept, it can be a kind of compass throughout the development process. Like a logline, it can also be descriptive. There's really no way to overemphasize the importance of a good title. It can motivate an investor to read your screenplay, and later it can entice a potential audience member to choose your film over the one playing down the street.

Hollywood studios prefer short, generic titles that don't get in the way of massive marketing campaigns. *Click. Cars. Crossover. Open Season. Lucky You. Happy Feet.* These simple titles attract interest and gain impact only because tens of millions of dollars in advertising and promotion are supporting them. Chances are you won't have that kind of money to promote your film. So you need to follow the model of independent filmmakers and come up with a title that generates interest entirely on its own. *Women on the Verge of a Nervous Breakdown. The Heart Is Deceitful Above All Things. Mini's First Time. The Oh in Ohio. I Am a Sex Addict.* When you see a title like any of these, you want to know, at the very least, more about the film that goes with it.

For some reason, many screenwriters struggle with titles. Perhaps it's the pressure of cramming everything they know about a screenplay into two or three words. If you find that you're one of those screenwriters, there's only one thing to do: stop worrying and come up with something—anything. Even a **working title** is better than no title. It will still help you to focus your ideas during the development process, and it will get you that much closer to coming up with a permanent title more to your liking. And the sooner you have any title, the better. By the time you develop your concept, you should have some sort of title attached to your project.

Buzz Word

Working title: A title given with the understanding that it's only provisional.

A premise, a concept, and a title are all public stages in the development process. You can use them not only to develop your screenplay but also to explain your work-in-progress to others. But, at this point in the development process, there comes a private stage, something not for public consumption but useful in the creation of your screenplay. That is a character interview.

Smart Quote

> "Often I'll find clues to where the story might go by figuring out where the characters would prefer not to go."
>
> Doug Lawson, short story writer

Character Interview

Remember that, to a great degree, the protagonist's choices and actions determine the dramatic action in your screenplay. Creating those choices and actions can often be a challenge, even when you already know the basic components of the concept: protagonist, super-objective, obstacle. A character interview helps to structure the process of discovery for you.

Let's be clear. A character interview is not the same as a character biography, which is often used by actors and writers. The problem with most character biographies is that they deal with details that have little impact on the direction of the story. A character interview focuses specifically on a character within the context of the plot for a screenplay.

To start, "ask" your protagonist these ten questions:

- What is your name?
- How would you describe yourself in three words?
- How would the other characters in the story describe you?
- What are you trying to accomplish in the screenplay that I am writing about you?
- What plan have you created to achieve your goal?
- Why is someone trying to stop you from achieving your goal? (What does that character have to lose or gain?)
- What will happen if you don't achieve your goal?
- How would you feel about that outcome?
- Will that feeling affect your choices and actions in the story?
- How does this story represent a pivotal moment in your life?

Because this is a private stage in the development process, there's no correct format for completing the interview. You can simply go through and respond to each question. Or you can put the responses together in a first-person narrative. Or you can write a third-person account of the interview, as if you were writing a newspaper or magazine article. The important thing is the information that the interview provides. After you complete the character interview with your protagonist, you may want to create a second interview, that one with your antagonist.

Once you have a familiarity with your protagonist and antagonist, you should begin to develop some sense of the overall movement of the story. For that, you need a synopsis.

In Focus: Character Interview

Because the character interview is a private stage in the development process, its precise form is up to the screenwriter. In a character interview for the screenplay "Coming In," screenwriter Vinnie Nguyen chose a simple question-and-answer format.

Q. What is your name?

A. My name is Brandon LaBlanc.

Q. Describe yourself in three words.

A. Well-meaning, caring, selfless.

Q. How would the other characters in the story describe you?

A. Stubborn, worrisome, deceptive.

Q. What are you trying to accomplish in the story that I am writing about you?

A. I'm trying to retain the guise of a gay teenager when in fact I'm straight.

Q. What plan have you created to achieve your goal?

A. A carefully constructed web of lies, deceit, and deception.

Q. Why is someone trying to stop you from achieving your goal? (What does that character have to lose or gain?)

A. My girlfriend wants us to be open about our relationship. My best friend is also sick of pretending to be my boyfriend.

Q. What will happen if you don't achieve your goal?

A. My gay dads will be disappointed that their only son is straight.

Q. How would you feel about that outcome?

A. The feeling of disappointing someone close to you is one of the worst feelings in the world.

Q. Will that feeling affect your choices and actions in the story?

A. Of course. People will do anything to protect someone they love from disappointment.

Q. How does this story represent a pivotal moment in your life?

A. In this story, I learn to accept who I am, no matter what the consequences may be.

Synopsis

A synopsis is a concise version of a *story* (not a plot) told in three to five paragraphs. Typically, the paragraphs are double-spaced, and the entire synopsis is no more than a page or two in length. If your synopsis is longer than two pages or five paragraphs, you're simply including too much detail in it. At this stage in the development process, you should be focusing on the overall direction of the story, and that's all.

The first paragraph in a synopsis corresponds to the setup. In it, you introduce the protagonist, that character's super-objective and need (if there is one), the antagonist, that character's super-objective and need (if there is one), and the inciting incident for the plot. You also convey some sense of the tone of the piece—that is, whether your screenplay will be funny or tragic, realistic or fantastic, etc. Sometimes, the style of writing in the synopsis will suggest the tone of the screenplay. When it doesn't, you should come right out and state it.

The middle paragraph(s) correspond to the rising action. Here, you deal with the obstacle(s) your protagonist faces in pursuit of the super-objective and how he overcomes them. The exact number of middle paragraphs will be determined by the complexity of the story. A synopsis for a short-short will have just one middle paragraph, while a synopsis for a long short might have as many as three.

In the closing paragraph, you address the screenplay's climax and resolution and the way in which they affect the characters generally and the protagonist in particular.

Remember that a synopsis is a brief description of a much larger, richer work. You're only suggesting what the final version of the screenplay will turn out to be and how you plan to accomplish it. Also remember that many of your ideas may—and probably will—change as you continue to work on your screenplay. So don't be afraid to improvise and experiment in this or any other stage of development.

In Focus: Synopsis

Earlier in this chapter, you read the character interview for "Coming In." This is the synopsis that developed from that interview.

> Brandon LeBlanc is having the time of his life at the Duke Ellington High School for the Arts. He's a straight-A student who's talented with both a paintbrush and a violin. Popular and easy on the eyes, he's enjoying life with his loyal best friend Casey and his adoring girlfriend Lisa. Everything seems picture-perfect. But there's just one problem. His fathers think he's gay.

> Ever since his dads, Mike and Brian, discovered his passion for art and classical music, they assumed and celebrated the fact that he was gay. Not wanting to ruin their joy, he has pretended to be gay to keep his fathers happy. After a few years, he's perfected the ruse.

> But tonight is the Junior Prom. Lisa wants to be known as more than just a friend to Brandon's parents, and Casey is sick of pretending to be his boyfriend. Convincing them to reprise their roles for one more night, Brandon must make a decision when his dads unexpectedly show up at the dance and catch him in a compromising position with Lisa.

Step Outline

So far, the development process has focused on story. With a step outline, development shifts to plot. A step outline—also known as a *beat sheet*—is a scene-by-scene outline of the major beats in a screenplay and the locations where those scenes take place. Like a character interview, it's a private stage of development, seldom viewed by anyone other than the screenwriter.

To create a step outline, you begin by identifying the location where the first beat occurs with a **scene heading**: for example, INT. CLASSROOM - DAY. Next, below that, in no more than a sentence, you state the *single main action in the scene*. You then repeat this process until you reach the resolution of your plot.

Buzz Word

Scene heading: The element of the formatted screenplay that indicates the location of the scene and the time of day that it takes place. Also known as a slug line.

Ultimately, every scene has one central action. There may be many other things happening in the scene, but they are either in service of or peripheral to that major beat. It's absolutely critical that you be able to identify the single action that drives a scene. If you can't or if you feel that there are actually two or three major beats, then you don't know what the scene is about. Equally important is your ability to express that central action in a single sentence. This forces you to reduce the scene to its essence, something that will be especially useful later, if, when you're writing a draft, a scene begins to meander and go "off-story."

Note

Bridge scenes are not dramatic and should never be included in a step outline.

A step outline for a five-page screenplay usually has three or four major beats, while a step outline for a ten-page screenplay has between five and eight. This means that, if you're writing either a short-short or a conventional short, your step outline allows you to see the entire plot on one computer screen or a single piece of paper. This is a tremendous advantage not only when you're forming the plot but also when you're actually writing a draft.

Naturally, longer screenplays require longer step outlines. For example, a 60-page screenplay might have 25–35 beats. This is not exact, though. Your results may vary.

In Focus: Step Outline

Earlier in this chapter, you read the character interview and the synopsis for "Coming In." This is the step outline that evolved from those stages in the development process. Notice that minor beats and bridge scenes, while essential in a draft of the screenplay, are not included in the step outline.

"COMING IN"

INT. SCHOOL - DAY

With the prom just a few hours away, BRANDON and LISA discuss his refusal to tell his parents that he's not gay.

EXT. SCHOOL - DAY

As CASEY walks home with Brandon, he's persuaded to play the role of Brandon's significant other once again, much to his dismay.

INT. HOUSE - LIVING ROOM - DAY

Brandon continues the charade of being gay for his gay parents, MIKE and BRIAN, while discussing his plans for the dance.

INT. BRANDON'S BEDROOM - NIGHT

Brandon prepares for the dance while ...

INT. LIVING ROOM - NIGHT

Casey plays his too familiar role as Brandon's significant other for Mike and Brian.

EXT. SCHOOL - NIGHT

Brandon meets up with Lisa as Casey pursues his own love interest.

INT. HOUSE - NIGHT

Mike and Brian realize that Brandon has left his cell phone at home and rush to the school to give it to him.

> INT. SCHOOL - NIGHT
>
> When Mike and Brian catch Brandon and Lisa in a compromising situation, the teenager is forced to admit his secret: he's not gay.
>
> EXT. SCHOOL - NIGHT
>
> After much hesitation, Mike and Brian admit their own secret: all along, they suspected that Brandon was straight.

Scene Outline

A scene outline is essentially a step outline with most, if not all, the minor beats included. As with a step outline, you begin writing a scene outline by identifying the location where the first beat occurs with a slug line. Then, below that, you lay out the minor beats for the scene in the form of either a list or a paragraph.

In the step outline for "Coming In," here's the way the first scene reads:

> INT. SCHOOL - HALLWAY - DAY
>
> With the prom just a few hours away, BRANDON and LISA discuss his refusal to tell his parents that he's not gay.

In a scene outline, here's the way that same scene reads:

> INT. SCHOOL - HALLWAY - DAY
>
> On the day of the prom, LISA tries to convince BRANDON to tell his gay parents that he's really straight so that the two teens can enjoy the dance as boyfriend and girlfriend. He refuses, fearing that his parents would freak out at the news. She argues that they are supportive people and that they would accept him for the straight person he is. He relents, agreeing to tell his parents soon...but not today.

There are two advantages to writing a scene outline. First, it provides you with a very thorough understanding of the content and the context of each scene. Second, because you know exactly what's going to happen, minor beat by minor beat, it expedites the writing process when you finally begin your first draft.

Sequence Outline

A sequence is a series of scenes connected by a single idea. That idea may be thematic, structural, or character-centered in nature. One of the most famous sequences in American film is the opening to *The Godfather*. There, the idea that connects the scenes is the wedding of Connie, the daughter of Don Corleone. Throughout the sequence, many characters are introduced, and a way of life is revealed. The action shifts from the boisterous celebration outdoors to the more subdued meeting of the don and others in his study. Still, every scene reflects the controlling idea of the sequence: the wedding.

Like a scene, a sequence is structurally a microcosm of the larger screenplay. It has its own setup, rising action, and climax. Because of this three-part structure, a sequence must be at least three scenes long, although some sequences are considerably longer than that. Naturally, with multiple scenes, a sequence will have a central action that's more complex than that of any single scene within it.

A sequence outline is simply a list of the sequences that will make up the action of the screenplay. Because this stage of development is private and intended for your eyes only, you can be as elaborate or as basic as you choose in the amount of information that you present. In fact, you may require no more than a word or two to communicate to yourself the controlling idea for each sequence. If you were describing the first sequence in *The Godfather*, for example, you might just write, "The Wedding."

In the development process, sequence outlines precede step outlines. One way of arriving at a step outline is to go through each sequence and decide which scenes are necessary to make it work. A medium short usually has two sequences and occasionally as many as four. A long short has five or more. Because of their brevity, short-shorts and conventional shorts essentially consist of just one sequence, so a sequence outline is of no value in developing a screenplay of that length.

In Focus: Sequence Outline

The long short "Life Lessons" has a running time of 44 minutes, and it consists of five sequences:

Lionel's World—Artist Lionel Dobie and his problems, personal and professional, are introduced.

More Turmoil—Against her better judgment, Paulette, Lionel's younger, live-in assistant, agrees not to move out of his loft, and the turmoil in their lives grows.

The Birthday Party—Lionel takes Paulette to an associate's birthday party where she hooks up with a handsome young artist, driving Lionel to despair.

The Performance Artist—Lionel convinces Paulette that she should stand up to an ex who dumped her, and the encounter ends in her public humiliation.

The End of the Affair—Lionel's overbearing ways finally drive Paulette out of his life for good.

Treatment

Traditionally, a treatment has been a 20–50-page prose version of the story for a screenplay. Over the years, though, this has evolved, and today the term is often used to describe any prose version of the story for a screenplay, regardless of its length. It's wise, then, that, if someone ever asks you to write a treatment, you be absolutely clear as to how many pages you expect to produce.

Obviously, a treatment of traditional length would be pointless in the development of a conventional short or a short-short. Why would you write 50 pages of prose when the screenplay itself is only five or ten pages long? However, a treatment of 20–25 pages might make sense for a long short, especially if you're tackling a difficult subject or a complicated story. Like a scene outline, a treatment provides you with a great deal of detail about story and character, which makes the writing process go faster and the drafts that you write better. Treatments are sometimes submitted to investors and producers, but, for the most part, such people prefer to read the screenplay itself.

Screenwriter's Notebook: What Will You Develop?

Not every screenwriter uses every stage of development because not every stage is equal in importance. Here are some guidelines.

Essential	Highly Desirable	Desirable	Focus
Premise			Story
Concept			Story
	Character interview		Story
	Synopsis		Story
Step outline			Plot
		Sequence outline	Plot
		Scene outline	Structure
		Treatment	Structure

First Draft

By now, you may be thinking, "With all this development, I'll never get around to actually writing the screenplay." Of course, you will. And when you do, you'll be totally prepared.

But don't let all your preparation close your mind to the many possibilities that will arise during the process of writing your first draft. Invariably, you'll come up with a line of dialogue or create an unplanned dramatic moment, and it will totally change the way you look at a scene or even your entire screenplay. Don't resist. Things change. Rather than worry that you're not following your step outline or scene outline exactly, take the inspiration of that new idea and let it lead you to even more discoveries. The fact is, if you don't make at least some changes to your original ideas, you're not allowing your screenplay enough room to grow.

As you remain open to new ideas, keep focused on the main goal of the first draft: *finishing it*. You always want to push toward the resolution and the moment that you can type the words "FADE OUT." Only then, when you reach the end, can you begin to assess the strengths and the weaknesses of your screenplay. Up to that point, you're like a sailor on the sea or a mountain climber on the ascent. What you see directly in front of you, whether a wall of rock or a roiling ocean or a page of a screenplay, doesn't tell you very much about how far you've come or how far you have left to go.

This leads to a quick word of advice about first drafts. Too many screenwriters feel the need to make each scene perfect before they can move onto the next one. What happens, though, is that, instead of perfecting the scene (which is impossible anyway), they paralyze themselves. They spend hour after hour rewriting a few lines of dialogue or some random scene directions. Resist the temptation to make each scene perfect, and just keep going. Get to the end. There will be time enough to fix things when you begin your revisions.

Revisions

There's a very human tendency to want to finish a screenplay, to be done with the thing, to say, "I've written this draft, and I'm not going to write anymore." Just remember that no one ever shot a film based on a first draft of anything. Never. Not once. That's because writing is a process of accumulation. You add layers of meaning and depth with each new pass that you take at the script. That goes for comedy as well as something more serious. And although your first draft may hold a lot of promise, promise alone is not something that should go before a camera.

After you finish your initial draft, the first thing to do is put it away in a drawer or in some well hidden folder on your hard drive. Leave it there, and don't take a look at it for a month or two or even more. Objectivity comes with distance, and you can't possibly develop either if you're looking at your screenplay every day.

Smart Quote

"I don't dawdle. I'm a surgeon. I make an incision, do what needs to be done, and sew up the wound."

Richard Selzer, essayist, short story writer

Once you're ready to go back to work, take a long and critical look at that first draft and begin to make notes on what you believe needs changing. At the same time, circulate the draft among people whose opinions you trust.

Be sure to let your readers know that you're really interested in hearing what that they have to say. And then, when they say it, make sure that you're really interested in hearing it. *Listen* to what people are telling you. Don't be defensive or dismissive. Challenging every comment that's made about your screenplay not only defeats the purpose of seeking criticism but also annoys people greatly.

You should always have more than one person read a draft because you're looking for patterns in the criticism and comments that you receive. If someone makes a particular criticism or comment, that deserves consideration. If two or more people make the same criticism or comment, that deserves *serious* consideration: you probably have a problem that needs addressing or a success that merits celebrating.

Note

Never give an early draft to someone who's not knowledgeable about filmmaking and screenwriting. Uninformed people are, well, uninformed. On the one hand, they could end up giving you criticism that's wrong, if not damaging. On the other hand, they might find perfection in a screenplay that's in serious need of revision.

Sometimes, the comments that you receive can be vague, and you need to be either a detective or a psychologist to understand what your reader is saying to you. Don't be afraid to ask questions. If you want to improve your screenplay, you need to know what the person is trying to get at.

Often, simply by isolating that part of the structure the comment applies to, you can begin to understand the nature of the comment. Here are some common trouble spots to look for.

Common problems in the setup

Too much time is spent creating the original world of the story.

Too much time is spent introducing the protagonist.

A number of scenes are used to illustrate a dramatic point that should be made in a single scene.

The inciting incident occurs too late.

Common problems in the rising action

There's not enough underlying story to generate the necessary plot.

There are not enough major beats, especially of a highly dramatic sort.

The conflict is not clearly articulated.

The protagonist and the antagonist are not evenly matched.

Common problems in the resolution

> The protagonist's character arc is unclear or unbelievable.
>
> The problems of the characters other than the protagonist are resolved too hastily or not at all.
>
> The major dramatic question is not answered satisfactorily.
>
> The minor dramatic question is not answered satisfactorily.

Principles of Rewriting

Change is frightening. It's especially frightening after you've spent so much time developing your ideas and writing your first draft. You've grown used to the way that your screenplay reads and looks. As a matter of fact, there are large parts of it that you genuinely like. Yet, the only way to make your second draft better than your first—and your third better than your second—is to embrace change.

- Be fearless. Every word is fair game for revision or excision.
- Shorten everything—dialogue, scene directions, entire scenes—everything.
- Save each day's work as a separate computer file. If you don't like what you've done, you can always go back.
- Keep a clear head. Don't discuss your current draft with anyone while you're actually writing it.
- Once you've finished a draft, put it away, and take some time off from it.
- The writing never stops. Even when your film is in production, you'll be polishing scenes and tweaking lines of dialogue.

Eventually, all the effort that you've expended on developing your ideas and all the hours that you've spent writing and rewriting will bring your screenplay to the point where it's ready for production. The demands on the screenplay and the screenwriter change once a film begins production. It's time to prepare yourself for that.

Chapter Five, Take Two—Chapter Review

▪ Characters, plot, setting, and theme each present you with a way to generate ideas for a screenplay.

▪ A *premise* is the dramatic situation from which the conflict arises and the action unfolds.

▪ A *concept* is the overall idea for a story (not a plot) expressed in one sentence, consisting of a protagonist, that character's super-objective, and the obstacle that stands in the way of attaining that objective.

▪ A *synopsis* is a concise prose version of a story (not a plot) told in three to five paragraphs.

▪ A *step outline*—also known as a beat sheet—is a scene-by-scene outline of the major beats that will make up the action in a screenplay.

▪ A *scene outline* is a more detailed scene-by-scene description of the screenplay, including most, if not all, of the minor beats that will make up the action in the screenplay.

▪ A *sequence outline* is a list of the sequences that will make up the action in a screenplay.

▪ Traditionally, a *treatment* has been a 20–50-page prose version of the story for a screenplay. Over the years, this has evolved, and today the term is often used to describe any prose version of the story for a screenplay, regardless of its length.

▪ Development is the process by which an idea for a film is broadened, refined, and improved.

▪ Prior to a first draft, there are eight stages of development: premise, concept, character interview, synopsis, step outline, scene outline, sequence outline, and treatment.

▪ Not all screenwriters use all eight stages. This is especially true in writing a short-short or a conventional short for which a sequence outline and a treatment are inappropriate.

▪ At the very least, you should create a concept, a synopsis, and a step outline before beginning your first draft.

▪ The main goal of a first draft is completing it. Only when you have reached the end, can you begin to assess the strengths and the weaknesses of your screenplay.

▪ Writing is a process of accumulation. Layers of meaning and depth are added with each new draft. You'll write many drafts of a screenplay before it's ready to go before the camera.

Chapter Six

Production

"Writing isn't as much fun when your life depends upon it."

Don Holley, screenwriter

Key Concepts

- Production realities and the screenplay
- Reducing production costs through rewriting
- Working as a part of the creative team

So far in the screenwriting process, you've been concerned primarily with your screenplay as a reading experience. You've been crafting words to convey the cinematic promise of your ideas. In the final analysis, though, a screenplay exists for just one reason: to be shot as a film.

When your project goes into **preproduction**, the entire approach to your work changes. You're no longer writing a screenplay—you're writing a film. Logistical and financial considerations begin to arise, and soon you find that your soaring artistic spirit is tempered by your inner accountant. This is doubly true if you're directing or producing the film.

> ### Buzz Word
>
> **Preproduction:** The planning stage in the filmmaking process, a time when locations are scouted, sets are constructed, schedules and budgets are created, and the script is fine-tuned.

No matter the scope of a production, whether it's a Hollywood blockbuster or a modest student film, one universal truth holds true: when it comes to time and money, there's never enough of either. Of course, Hollywood studios have a little more latitude where matters of budget and schedule are concerned. (What's a few million dollars more when you've already burned

113

through eighty or ninety million?) You, on the other hand, don't have those resources. What you do have is creativity and foresight.

Well in advance of the start of **principal photography**, you need to know that not only is your screenplay dramatically effective, but it's also manageable—logistically and financially. Standing on the set is the last place that you want to discover that your script is too complicated or too expensive to shoot.

Buzz Word

Principal photography: The stage of the filmmaking process in which a film is shot. Often referred to simply as *production*.

Although preproduction can be a hectic time in the life of a film, it's still considerably calmer than principal photography. Think of the making of a film as a very long freight train. During preproduction, the train is pulling out of the station, gradually gathering momentum despite its great weight. By the time principal photography begins, it's hurtling down the mountainside, and no one seems to know where the brakes are.

Principal photography is, quite simply, a time for only the most basic or essential changes in a screenplay. There are too many other aspects of the production that require attention. In preproduction, then, you have one last opportunity to think about your screenplay in relative calm and quiet. The calm and quiet is relative, though.

As you go over your script, look for elements and scenes that, realistically, you'll never have the resources to do properly. Nothing marks a film as the work of amateur like scenes that lack appropriate **production values**. Rewrite those scenes or cut them, but under no circumstances should you try to shoot them as written.

Buzz Word

Production values: A film's level of polish, determined by the quality of the image and sound, the elaborateness of the production design, the use of visual and special effects, and the degree of accomplishment in such craft areas as continuity and the blocking of extras. Although Hollywood films typically have high production values, budget alone doesn't determine that. A film with a sizeable budget might use low production values to achieve a desired dramatic effect.

You should also identify elements and scenes that are doable but only at a considerable expense of time and money. Shooting flashy, attention-grabbing scenes—the so-called "candy of moviemaking"—is tempting. But the success of a film is never the result of a single scene. And the failure of a film could be, especially if that one scene puts such a tremendous demand on resources that it breaks the budget and destroys the shooting schedule.

Pitfalls and Money Pits

Before your project enters preproduction, you're essentially writing in a fantasyland. You sit at your computer, typing blissfully away, laboring in the perfect world of your imagination where everything works out exactly the way you expect. Everything. Every line, every gesture, every location, every set piece. Savor the version of the film that plays inside your head. It has an audience of one—you.

The reality is that shooting a film is an exercise in encountering limitations, facing problems, and finding acceptable compromises. Rather than viewing this as a drawback, though, you should embrace it for what it is: an opportunity to be as creative as you can possibly be. In the course of making your film, you'll have many opportunities to be creative in the face of limitation. Here's an overview.

Smart Quote

"Don't write what you know. Write what you own."

Rick Schmidt, low-budget film producer

Too Many Roles

Earlier in this book, you saw that, from a story perspective, a large cast of characters is never a particularly good thing in a short film. Narrative concerns aside, though, there are also important practical reasons for limiting cast size.

As with any group effort, the more people there are involved in the production of a film, the greater the likelihood of personal differences and conflicts. A larger cast will naturally bring more people into your project. They may all be talented actors and wonderful human beings. Of course, they may all be talented actors and not so wonderful human beings, too. A small cast made up of only the most essential roles certainly doesn't eliminate the possibility of personnel problems, but it does reduce the chances.

A large cast is also expensive. Undoubtedly, you realize that each member of the cast, including extras, will require specific wardrobe and make-up. That takes money, even if clothes are bought at a thrift shop and make-up is shared. What you may not realize is that there are also less obvious costs associated with a cast. Each actor will require transportation to and from the set. If an actor provides his own transportation, he'll expect reimbursement for gas, tolls, and parking. On any day that a shoot lasts more than a few hours, each actor on the set will need to be fed. And if the shoot takes place at a remote location, there's the expense of housing. These costs can add up quickly, especially when they are multiplied for a large cast.

In Focus: Craft Services

Napoleon Bonaparte famously observed, "An army travels on its stomach." The same can be said for a movie crew. If people are working for little or no money on your film, one way to keep them happy is to keep them fed. Large commercial productions always have a caterer on hand, serving meals at mealtime and then setting out buffet-style spreads known as *craft services tables* throughout the rest of the production day. You certainly don't need anything as elaborate as a caterer on your set, but you should set up a craft services table, even if it just contains snacks for "grazing." The crew will appreciate the food, but they will also appreciate the respect that this sort of consideration shows them.

At this point, you may be thinking that you might cut some corners by putting your friends in the cast. Despite its obvious appeal, you should think long and hard about casting friends, even if they are experienced actors. First, there's no guarantee that they will be right for the roles available, and it's more important that you cast suitable actors rather than put some pals on the screen. Second, your friends will be doing you a favor by appearing in your film, which may come back to haunt you. There's a limit to the amount of time that even best friends will give up for what is your project and not theirs. It's far better to cast actors who have no history with you and who are absolutely committed to appearing in your film. Third, when you're making a film, you don't really want friends; you want collaborators. The atmosphere on the set should be relaxed, but not so relaxed that your actors behave as if they are hanging out with you in your living room.

In Focus: Using Professional Actors

One cost that can be totally avoided in the production of a short film is actors' salaries. The fact is that you don't necessarily have to offer a salary to attract a good actor, even a professional one. Many actors are looking for performances to add to their demo reels, and they are willing to take an interesting role in a short film in exchange for a DVD copy of it. Members of the Screen Actors Guild, the union of professional screen actors, are allowed to perform for a deferred salary if a film is 35 minutes or shorter and if its budget is $50,000 or less. This means that they make money only if the film does. These actors *do* need to be treated as professionals, and so they should never be out of pocket for the expenses that they incur while performing in a film.

For complete details on using actors who are members of the Screen Actors Guild, consult the union's relevant web page: http://www.sagindie.org/contracts.html

---

Critters

Well-trained animals are everywhere in big-budget commercial films. Like any good actor, they make it look easy. Don't be fooled. The animals that you see on the screen labor long hours with professional trainers in order to perform on cue.

Desperate to get a particular animal character into a film, more than a few filmmakers have succumbed to the temptation of using family pets. Working with untrained animals is a dicey proposition, even if you're not asking your pet to be the De Niro of animal acting. Simply hitting a mark or vocalizing on cue may require so many takes for an untrained animal performer that your shooting schedule could be thrown into serious disarray.

As cute as animals are, you should resist including them in your screenplay right from the start. But if there's already an animal in your script, pre-production is the perfect time to cut the critter. Everyone, including the animal in question, will thank you for it.

Kids

Posing even greater problems than animals are children. State labor laws strictly limit both the hours and the conditions of their work. (And don't think for a minute that, just because they're not getting paid, they're not working.) In most states, a child can work just four hours a day, which is not much in the filmmaking world where twelve- to sixteen-hour days are the norm. If the child is of school age and school is in session, he'll need a tutor on the set.

Joining the child on the set will be a parent (or legal guardian), who must be present at all times. So you're casting not just a child but also the adult that comes with him—a package deal. That adult may have very different ideas from yours about what the child is capable of or what he should be doing on camera or even when he should go home for the day. Never underestimate the stress that comes with a dissatisfied stage mother or stage father.

In Focus: A Child Actor's Workday

Have you ever noticed in a film's credits that the role of an infant or a toddler has two or three names after it? That's because twins and sometimes triplets are hired to play a single role, four hours at a time. In that way, a full day of shooting can take place without violating child labor laws.

Most truly talented child actors work regularly and get paid good money for it, so there's a very real possibility that the children available for your film will have more ambition than experience. With so much to be done in the course of a day in production, the last thing that anyone needs is to conduct on-the-job training in the craft of film acting. And keep in mind that even "professional children"—children who have professional acting careers—are still children. They have their good days when they are mature and responsible, and they have their bad days when they behave like visitors from another planet.

If you haven't gotten the message by now, children, like animals, are best left to filmmakers with deep pockets, large crews, and endless reserves of patience. Preproduction presents the final opportunity to cut all children from your script. You should take advantage of it.

Stunts

Although people tend to think of stunts as something spectacular—high falls and car crashes, say—a stunt is any physical action that could *conceivably* endanger a member of the cast or the crew. That may be something as simple as an actor falling backward, even onto something as inviting as a bed.

Because there's the possibility of physical harm coming to someone and because the risky action must be performed convincingly, a scene with a stunt always requires more time to shoot than a scene without one. And that's true no matter how elementary the stunt may look on paper. What's more, scenes involving a series of stunts—fight scenes, for example—require not only more shooting time but also more editing time, which has an impact on both production and post-production schedules.

Serious stunts—those that, if done wrong, could result in someone's hospitalization or worse—should never be taken lightly. They should be created and supervised by a professional stunt coordinator. In addition, a professional stunt performer may be needed as a **stunt double**. Will your production have the time and money for all that? Only you can say for certain. But never do things on the cheap when someone's health and well-being is at stake.

Buzz Word

Stunt double: A stunt performer who assumes the role of a cast member in the performance of a stunt.

Nudity

Even when actors are paid lots of money, they are generally reluctant to take off their clothes in public. So you can imagine their eagerness to strip when they are getting paid nothing (or something close to it). You may get lucky and find an exhibitionist who's ready to take off his clothes at the drop of a hat. You may also win the Nobel Prize in Physics. The odds are about the same.

Of course, you could hire a **body double**, but you'll end up paying for the privilege. Earning money is about the only reason that someone accepts that kind of work. But using a double won't make the shooting go faster. Blocking will still need to be handled with a great deal of sensitivity, and the set will still be closed to all but the most essential personnel, causing the work of shooting the scene to go more slowly.

Like a scene with a stunt, a scene with nudity always takes longer to shoot than one without it. And time, as the saying goes, is money.

Buzz Word

Body double: A performer who takes the place of a featured actor in a scene that requires nudity or unusual physical fitness.

Even fully clothed, some actors have difficulty with scenes of intimacy. That passionate kiss that took you just a few seconds to write could take up an entire morning of shooting as the two actors struggle to convey some sense of authenticity in their relationship. Which leads to another, related point…

"Scenery Chewing"

In very short order, the pages of your script will become **sides** that actors will perform. Fix a critical eye on any moment that places unusual acting demands on your cast. Although you may not want to eliminate that beat or scene, you may consider softening it.

Hysterical crying, uncontrollable laughter, and blind rage are typical of moments that are compelling on paper but truly problematic in performance. An actor who doesn't totally commit himself to these kinds of moments or simply doesn't have the talent to play them persuasively makes your film and your writing look amateurish. Unfortunately, there's no way to know whether someone can make a scene work until it's performed, which is generally too late for you to do anything about it. More often than not, you do your film a great service by writing with understatement.

Buzz Word

Scenery chewing: Slang for an overly dramatic acting performance, especially one that comes off as overacting.

Sides: Script pages for a particular scene, often distributed on five-and-a-half-inch by eight-inch paper so that an actor or a director can hold them comfortably in one hand while rehearsing or blocking.

Locations (too many)

One of the goals in producing a short film is to use the fewest locations possible. That's because moving from one location to another takes up time better spent actually shooting the film.

Moving also adds expense, even if everyone on the production is working for free. Simply using a location sometimes requires paying a fee to either the person or the company that owns it. But even when there's no charge, there's the cost of dressing the location to look the way the director and the production designer envision it. Getting to the location has a price, too, in transportation costs for the crew and cast. Invariably, in any production, some equipment will need to be rented, and those charges will increase in direct relation to the length of the shooting schedule.

For a short film with a modest budget, a good rule of thumb is to plan for one location per shooting day. So, for example, a screenplay with two locations would require a shooting schedule of at least two days, a screenplay with three locations would require at least three days, and so on. Naturally, the exact number of days at any given location depends on the total number of pages to be shot there.

The best and easiest way to limit the number of locations is at the conceptual level: devise a plot that requires just a handful of them. Ideally, you should center the action at a primary location that accounts for at least half the pages of the screenplay. This allows for multiple days at that single location, a real boon in allowing everyone to focus on production rather than scheduling.

Even during preproduction, it's possible for a screenwriter to adjust the screenplay so that fewer locations are required. Just go through the script and look for scenes whose content isn't inextricably linked to a specific place. There are probably more of these scenes in your screenplay than you're aware of. Once you've identified a scene of this kind, shift its location to one used elsewhere in the screenplay. In all likelihood, you won't have to change more than a line or two of dialogue to accommodate the shift.

Other scenes to look out for are short ones—a quarter page or a half page in length—occurring in a location used only once in the entire production. These scenes will prove to be a scheduling headache. Cut them if you can. If not, rewrite them for an existing location already used in other scenes. Ultimately, you're aiming to create enough scenes at each location so that at least one entire shooting day can be spent there.

To make your screenplay even less of a logistical challenge, write with specific locations in mind, places that you're personally familiar with, ones that will permit access to your production and will accommodate the size of the crew working on your film. As you're considering potential locations, try to identify those that can also double for other locations in the script. For example, with minimal set dressing and the right camera angles, a house with a front yard and a back yard can serve as two distinct locations. Likewise, two rooms in the same house can pass for totally separate places simply by preceding each scene with an establishing shot of a different exterior.

Locations (too public)

Concern about locations is not strictly in the numbers. Certain kinds of places are almost always problematic as film locations, so they are best avoided in your screenplay.

Public streets or sidewalks are perfect for getting you from one place to another but nightmarish for shooting. Public access has to be controlled, requiring at least one crew member to direct traffic. In extreme cases, an off-duty police officer may need to be hired. Owners whose buildings front the street or sidewalk must give their permission, which is often dependent upon the payment of a location fee.

For a sense of realism in a street or sidewalk scene, **extras** will have to be used, which means more crew will be needed to supervise them, more food will be needed to feed them, and more vehicles will be needed to transport them. And that assumes that you'll even be able to find extras to appear in your film. You can entice an actor to work for free with the promise of getting his performance captured on DVD. What can you offer an extra?

Buzz Word

Extra: A non-specific, non-speaking performer, typically appearing in the background of a scene or as a part of a crowd.

Moving a production from outdoors to indoors can present its own set of problems. Specialized locations like hospital rooms, doctor's examining rooms, and funeral homes are often difficult to secure, and dressing another location to look like one of these places will require enough specialty equipment to add significantly to your production budget.

Certain publicly owned public spaces should essentially be considered off-limits. Government buildings, schools, courthouses, airports, and train stations are very difficult to secure as locations for reasons ranging from homeland security to bureaucratic entrenchment.

Privately owned public spaces, like stores, restaurants, and other places of business, can be secured but not without effort. Very few proprietors will allow a production to shoot during normal business hours because of the income that will be lost. As a result, shooting will have to take place after hours, usually overnight, which isn't a particularly inviting prospect. The cast and crew can get very cranky at four o'clock in the morning.

Vehicles

Because the major film studios are in California and California is a car culture, cars are popular in Hollywood films. Often, the make of a car that a character drives provides a shorthand for his identity. Cars are also popular in some television series because their interiors offer an easy location for heavy dialogue scenes that might otherwise be shot on a street or a sidewalk where track would have to be laid for a tracking shot and public access would have to be controlled.

You, on the other hand, should steer clear of cars or any similarly sized vehicle like a pickup truck. Aesthetically, shooting inside a car is extremely limiting because there are few available camera angles and therefore few visual possibilities. Practically, it's costly and time-consuming. Special equipment like a camera-car is necessary, as is a specially trained camera operator. Consideration must be given to every aspect of the travel route right down to the road surface: what's the likelihood of finding a street without a single bump or pothole in the area where the film is in production? Additionally, in many locales, shooting a moving vehicle requires a police escort.

Other types of vehicles also present problems. Beyond the obvious technical hurdles involved in shooting on a bus or a train, renting either is probably well beyond the budget of most short films. Shooting an airplane interior usually requires renting a cabin or cockpit mockup. The availability of these sets is limited, and their rental cost is high. Official vehicles like police patrol cars and specialty vehicles like taxis and ice cream trucks can be rented, but only in those areas of the country where there's enough production activity to sustain a company that rents vehicles to the film industry. Anywhere else, a producer has to be extremely resourceful or just plain lucky.

If a scene inside a vehicle exists in your script at the time of preproduction, shift it to another, stationary location.

Weapons

Weapons, from a storytelling perspective, are rarely an imaginative addition to a screenplay. In fact, their omnipresence in commercial feature films can turn them into something of a cliché in short films. If that isn't reason enough to cut every weapon from your script, the practicalities of life on the set should be.

Scenes involving guns or rifles require the services of a licensed gun handler (and in some locales a police officer, too). On a bigger budget film, the person handling firearms may be the special effects coordinator or a member of the art department. For a short film with a small crew, someone will have to be hired specifically for this job.

If you've written a scene in which the gun is actually fired and the shots "hit" their target, you'll need a special effects artist to wire and fire the **squibs**. (That person may also be the gun handler.) As with stunts, creating bullet hits should always be left to professionals, people with experience and liability insurance. Using homemade charges could result in serious bodily harm to either the actor wearing the squibs or the person wiring them.

Knives and swords present less of a logistical concern than guns and rifles, although clearly they must be handled with care. Keep in mind that certain exotic knives, as well as certain exotic firearms, may be totally illegal in the particular jurisdiction where a film is shooting.

Buzz Word

Squib: A blood pack taped to a small explosive charge, which sits atop a padded plate that protects the actor wearing it. A remote triggering device fires the squib, spraying a blood-like substance.

Weather

Who doesn't love atmospheric touches like the terrifying thunderstorm featured in almost every horror flick or the blinding snowstorm that's a fixture of every outdoor adventure? Well, producers don't.

Weather costs money. Real money. It's a special effect, created on the set through no small expenditure of labor, equipment, and money. Rain, even a gentle mist, requires a rain tower, a water truck, and people who know how to operate each. Snow is technically more demanding, requiring a snow machine, a wind machine, supplies of simulated snowflakes and snow powder, and people who know how to pull all that together. The irony is that, whenever weather effects are created, the actual weather outside must be perfect without a hint of wind or any real precipitation. Even then, the look of artificial rain or snow won't be consistent from take to take.

Of course, you could hold out for the real thing. But, clearly, Mother Nature has never produced a film. Expect not only to do a lot of waiting for the desired meteorological conditions but also to encounter major **continuity** problems when the weather does arrive. Rain, for example, may be torrential in one take and barely a drizzle in another.

Buzz Word

Continuity: Consistency in the details of a scene—makeup, wardrobe, lighting, set dressing, special effects—that allows different takes to be cut together to provide the illusion of continuous action.

So whether the weather is real or man-made, you're better off without it. The best strategy? Never write a scene that depends in any way on weather conditions, good or bad.

Clearances

Have you ever noticed that, at birthday parties in films, when the cake is brought out, characters will break into a rousing rendition of "For He's a Jolly Good Fellow"? When was the last time you sang "For He's a Jolly Good Fellow" at a birthday party? So why do characters in films do that? Do they all have an odd taste in music?

The answer is simple—copyright protection. The rights to "Happy Birthday" are owned by a publishing company, which expects payment for the use of its property. "For He's a Jolly Good Fellow" is in the **public domain**, so its use is free for all.

Public domain: The body of creative works and inventions to which no person or entity has any claim of legal ownership.

Intellectual property law is complicated and far-reaching, and this book isn't the appropriate forum for an in-depth, authoritative discussion of it. Still, as a screenwriter and a filmmaker, you have to understand that much of popular culture—songs, logos, commercials—is legally owned by someone, and you can't simply appropriate whatever you choose in your work. The lesson that you learned in kindergarten still holds true today: don't take things that don't belong to you.

And just what doesn't belong to you? Pretty much everything that doesn't come directly out of your imagination. There are the obvious things: lines from television shows, images from films, lyrics from songs. But there are also less obvious things: company logos, advertising tag lines, magazine and book covers. To include any of these things in your film, you'll need a **clearance**.

Clearance: Express permission given by the owner of copyright- or trademark-protected material for its inclusion in a film.

The commonest element needing clearance in a film is music. Whether it's playing softly on a radio in the background or turned up full for the title sequence, whether a character is humming a recognizable tune or quoting song lyrics in a line of dialogue, permission must be obtained from its owner for you to use it in a film.

Because short films generally make little or no money, one solution is to seek a festival waiver. This form of permission grants the filmmakers the legal right to include music in a film for a limited time, provided that no money will be earned from the screening of the film. (That's why this permission is called a *festival* waiver—as in film festival.) The good news is that you can generally obtain this kind of permission for a token payment or in some cases no payment at all. The bad news is that, because a music company stands to make so little money from the deal, its legal department is going to be very slow to respond to your request.

Screenwriter's Notebook: Items Requiring Clearance

This list isn't meant to be exhaustive, but it should give you an idea of the sorts of things requiring clearance.

- Lyrics to songs
- Music to songs
- Performances of songs
- Clips from other films
- Clips from television shows
- Computer screenshots
- Book covers
- Text from books
- Magazine covers
- Newspaper front pages
- Text from magazine or newspaper articles
- Photographs
- Works of art created by living or recently deceased artists
- Logos
- Print advertisements
- Radio and television commercials
- Any trademarked product: cell phones, MP3 players, computers, musical instruments, kitchen appliances, farm machinery—if it has a company's name on it and the audience can read the logo, you need to obtain a clearance

Needless to say, it's up to you to find out who actually owns the music that you're interested in using, a task that could be complicated and time-consuming. But make no mistake: no matter how much of a piece of music you intend to use, you must obtain permission for it. There's absolutely no truth to the urban legend that, if you include fewer than eight bars of music, you don't need permission for its use.

Even more challenging than acquiring the rights to music is acquiring the rights to other forms of recorded media. If you're considering using a clip from a previously produced film or a television show, you'll run into the same legal hurdles as clearing music, plus some added costs. In addition to the fee owed the copyright owner (usually a movie studio or a television network), you'll have to pay residuals to the director, the screenwriter, and the actors appearing in the clip.

Given the expense and the legal considerations involved in obtaining permissions, you should never specify a particular song cue or media clip in your screenplay. Even more important, you should never build an entire scene around either. If the scene is shot and you end up unable to secure the necessary rights, the only place that you'll be able to screen your film without the threat of legal action is in the comfort of your own home.

And don't take the attitude that, because you don't have much in the way of financial assets, you're not worth suing. Lawyers are funny about getting their way. They will find someone who does have assets and put the squeeze on that person—say, the director of a film festival. Rest assured that the mere threat of legal action will keep your film out of circulation.

Working with Others

The way that you approach your screenplay during preproduction and production will depend on the other position or positions that you hold on the production team. If you're responsible for the screenplay alone, your approach will be different from that if you're also the director and/or the producer.

As a screenwriter collaborating with a director, you can expect the most serious discussions about your screenplay to take place before the start of preproduction. Every screenplay brings with it a unique set of circumstances, but generally anything is open to consideration and possible revision at this stage. Characters, plot developments, the structure of individual scenes, the amount of dialogue (too much or too little)—all come under scrutiny when the screenwriter and the director begin their collaboration. Discussions about what should be cut from the screenplay, what should remain, and what should remain but with modifications are among the most difficult in the making of any film. You must strike a balance between protecting your ideas and collaborating with others.

In all likelihood, a film will go into preproduction only if the director and the producer are confident that the script is in reasonably good shape or that real progress is being made toward mutually agreed upon goals. Once preproduction starts, you'll meet regularly with the director—and sometimes the producer as well—to discuss the revisions that you've been making. Generally, a screenwriter turns in revised pages as he completes a scene or two. This allows the crew members to avoid wasting time on planning scenes or parts of scenes that have changed substantially or no longer exist.

By the start of production, your work as a screenwriter may be done. Or it may not be. It's rare that even a shooting script will be shot exactly as written. Some directors are inclined to make all the script changes that occur during principal photography, everything from line tweaks made on the set to more elaborate revisions that need to be done once the crew has gone home for the night. Other directors focus exclusively on the production and urge their screenwriters to keep their cell phones on and within reach at all times during principal photography. Every director has different expectations, and every screenwriter has a different level of interest in continuing the collaboration.

Working with a director has its advantages. First, some screenwriters just want to write, and this allows them to do that. Second, a director brings a fresh perspective to a script, which can infuse it with new energy. Of course, there's a very clear disadvantage to having someone other than you direct your screenplay, and that is that someone other than you is directing your screenplay. You've spent all that time creating your dream only to hand it over to a director who may not share your vision. That's why most people who write short screenplays also direct them.

Directing your own screenplay isn't without its drawbacks, though. Yes, you're the person in charge, but that doesn't mean that you enjoy the same unchallenged supremacy as the dictator of a small country. On the contrary, you're collaborating with every member of the cast and crew, a collaboration that will prove far more complicated and time-consuming than if you were responsible for only the screenplay, especially since most everyone will be working for little or no money. That collaboration also includes regular and detailed meetings with your producer, whose focus is going to be distinctly nuts-and-bolts. And because you have so many responsibilities beginning the first day of preproduction, you need to make sure that your screenplay is in filmable shape well before then. That takes the form of a production draft.

Locking the Pages of a Script

The production draft is essentially your last complete pass at the script. Because this draft is circulated after preproduction begins, scenes need to be numbered for the first time, and any changes and deletions that are made after its initial distribution will need to be communicated to the crew and the cast. To ensure that the changes are communicated properly, you first must lock the pages of the script.

Like any word processing file, a script repaginates whenever text is added or deleted. This isn't a problem when you're sitting at your computer, writing your screenplay. However, once the production draft is circulated and your crew and cast have begun to make notations on their scripts as they go about their work, it's counterproductive to distribute an entirely new script whenever a scene or a few lines change.

Locking the script keeps each individual page consistent with preceding versions of that page. So no matter how much text is added to or deleted from any given page, the pages coming before and after remain unchanged. If there's so much new text that an additional page is required, that new page becomes an "A" page. If a second page is needed, that becomes a "B" page. And so on through the alphabet. On the other hand, if material is deleted, text from the following pages is not "brought up" from the following page to fill the gap. Instead, the page with the deleted text is left with open white space.

In Focus: Locked Pages

Say that you've added a lot of new dialogue to a scene that you've been revising. The scene, which used to end at the bottom of page 6, now spills onto the top third of the following page. If page 6 weren't locked, the new dialogue would appear on page 7 and, in doing so, would alter every page that follows in the screenplay. With the script pages locked, that new dialogue spills onto a brand new page, 6A, and page 7—as well as the rest of the pages—remains unchanged. Most screenwriting formatting software offers a menu option to lock pages. You can accomplish the same thing with any word processing software by inserting a page break at the bottom of each page of your production draft.

To ensure that your crew and cast are literally on the same page, you should change the information in the header of each revised page, indicating the date of the revision. This is especially important if you have certain pages that undergo multiple revisions. To add a touch of professionalism to your screenplay, you can distribute revised pages on colored paper with each set of revisions distributed in a different color.

Screenwriter's Notebook: "Pink Pages"

On professional movie sets, revised pages are always distributed on colored paper. These pages are referred to as "pink pages," even when they are of some other, entirely different, hue. The order in which colors are used for revised pages follows a basic pattern:

Pink

Blue

Green

Yellow

Orange

Buff

Tan

Goldenrod

Lavender

So that your production team is not wasting time searching for particular changes on a page, indicate any change, including deletions, with an asterisk in the right margin next to the changed line.

```
A brief beat and then she puts the book on    *
the nightstand, moves closer to Stephen,      *
then tenderly removes the headphones          *
from his ears.                                 *
```

Naturally, that line of text could be dialogue, a scene direction, a parenthetical direction, a character cue, a scene heading, even a transition. If an entire scene is deleted, the scene number remains in the script, and either the word "OMIT" or the word "CUT" appears in place of the scene heading.

Note

For a clearer idea of the use and placement of asterisks and scene numbers, look at the sample shooting script in Appendix D, "Sample Screenplay—Shooting Script."

A Brief Word about Rehearsal

Because short films so often lack adequate resources and personnel, rehearsals with the cast and the director may seem like a luxury. But making certain that your actors are fully prepared and that they have a complete understanding of your screenplay can hardly be considered a luxury. Actors who are comfortable with their material not only give better performances but they also make the production process go more smoothly.

Still, when time is at a premium as it so often is in preproduction, compromises are made, and rehearsals are among the first things given up. At the very least, though, there should be a **table reading** of the screenplay, preferably in the early days of preproduction. Listening to the cast read your lines, even if the reading is "cold," will give you a good idea whether your dialogue needs to be tweaked or entirely rewritten. Some problems you'll hear for yourself. Others will be pointed out by the actors and the director (if you're not directing the film yourself). Keep an open mind, and don't be defensive. Collaboration on a film requires extensive give and take.

Buzz Word

Table reading: A preliminary reading of a screenplay by the entire cast, usually with key members of the crew present. The use of the word *table* stems from the fact that such readings are generally conducted with actors sitting around a table.

Among the final responsibilities of the screenwriter during preproduction is ensuring that the screenplay conforms to the actual locations that have been secured. By and large, this is a straightforward process, involving minor adjustments. Sometimes, only the scene heading needs to be changed. Occasionally, the location is so different from what's suggested in the original screenplay, that scenes must be revised from top to bottom.

Once all the changes are made to the production draft and principal photography begins, the screenplay has evolved into a shooting script.

Chapter Six, Take Two—Chapter Review

- Once your project goes into preproduction, you're no longer writing a screenplay—you're writing a film.

- The process of shooting a film involves encountering limitations, facing problems, and finding acceptable compromises—all of which give you the opportunity to be more creative.

- In preproduction, you should rewrite or cut scenes that you'll never have the resources for. You should also cut or rewrite scenes that are doable but only at a considerable expense of time and money.

- A cast with many roles runs the risk of inflating the production budget and increasing the possibility of personality conflicts.

- Using children or animals in a film presents logistical challenges that can adversely affect the shooting schedule.

- Artificial weather—rain, snow, or wind—is expensive because its creation requires special equipment and specially trained operators.

- Certain kinds of public places, like streets and stores, can be problematic as film locations, so they are best avoided in a screenplay.

- Shooting inside a moving vehicle is costly and time-consuming while providing few possibilities for camera angles.

- Any physical action that could conceivably result in the injury of a member of the cast or crew is considered a stunt. Major stunts require a stunt coordinator and one or more stunt doubles.

- Firearms on the set require a licensed gun handler as well as a special effects artist to rig any firearms "hits."

- Much of popular culture—songs, television shows, commercials, logos—is legally owned by someone and can't be appropriated for use in a film without permission.

Chapter Seven

Format

"Nobody makes bad movies on purpose."

Roland Emmerich, screenwriter, director, producer

Key Concepts

- The elements of a formatted screenplay
- The standard industry format
- Special situations in screenplay form and format

Screenplays look a certain way on paper. By writing your screenplay in the standard industry format, you accomplish two things. One, you develop a reasonably good idea of the running time of the completed film based on your screenplay. (Remember that one page of a screenplay will equal about one minute of screen time in the edited film.) Two, because you're writing in a format that anyone knowledgeable about filmmaking is familiar with, readers are able to concentrate on the content of your screenplay and the strength of your ideas rather than the eccentricities of page layout.

There are some pretty basic ground rules in screenplay form and format.

1. Always write in the present tense.
2. Write in master scenes—leave shots and camera angles for a **shot list**.
3. Use the correct font: 12-point Courier.
4. When the time comes to print your screenplay, use three-hole punched paper, and bind it together with Acco $1^1/_4$-inch fasteners.
5. If you want to put a cover on your screenplay, use plain white card stock.

Buzz Word

Shot list: Developed by the director, a list that indicates the scenes scheduled for a shooting day. Usually included in each entry are the scene number, the location, a short description of the scene, the length of the scene in pages, a list of actors in the scene, and notes to departments of any special needs.

Note

If the Courier font isn't available on your computer—a problem with some PCs running Windows—try to use something close that's not Courier New, which is too large a font. A little searching on the Internet should turn up a suitable substitute.

Those are the basics. Naturally, there's more to script format than that, beginning with the six main elements of the formatted screenplay.

Scene Headings

A scene heading establishes the place and time of a scene. It begins with either INT. (short for interior—a scene taking place indoors) or EXT. (short for exterior—a scene outdoors), which is followed by the name of the actual location. Then comes a dash, usually typed as a hyphen, along with an indication of the time of day, which is either DAY or NIGHT. A complete scene heading looks like this:

```
EXT. PARK - DAY
```

Sometimes, the action spreads over a larger, expansive location that actually breaks down into smaller locations as the events unfold. In that case, a scene heading might be written like this:

```
EXT. PARK - POND - DAY
```

The pond is a more accurate description of the location of the scene because that's where the crew will set up. Without a mention of the park in the scene heading, though, the pond could be anywhere. The next scene in the sequence might have a scene heading like this:

```
EXT. PARK - BIKE PATH - DAY
```

As you may have noticed from these examples, articles (*the*, *a*, and *an*) are customarily left out of scene headings. You simply write "EXT. PARK" rather than "EXT. THE PARK" or "EXT. A PARK."

Keep in mind that the information included in a scene heading is production information, not narrative information. So don't include specific time references (mid-morning, 9:00 A.M., sunrise, Sunday, the first day of spring) or relative time references (two hours later, later that morning, the following day, continuous). If this information is important to the telling of your story, you'll have to find some other way to communicate it to an audience, who won't have an opportunity to read your scene headings as your film plays on the screen.

Scene Directions

Scene directions describe two things: the way a location looks and the action that occurs there.

Every scene must contain some scene directions, however brief. At the very least, you indicate which characters are on-screen at the beginning of the scene and what they are generally up to. You should never follow a scene heading directly with dialogue, even if logic dictates that the scene is a continuation of the previous one and that the cast of characters is the same in both. A scene without scene directions makes life difficult for everyone, especially the person breaking down your script and putting together a shooting schedule.

Only the briefest description should be used to establish a location, and some locations are so unimportant or commonplace that they need no description at all. If a scene takes place outside a convenience store, for example, and the store has no distinguishing features other than it's a store and it offers convenience, there's no point in wasting time setting up the location. "EXT. CONVENIENCE STORE" says all that you need to say about the place.

In writing scene directions, remember that a screenplay is not a novel or a short story. Describe only what an audience can see or hear or what an actor can play. This means that you should never include biographical data (Bob grew up in the suburbs of Cleveland) or specific non-visual ideas (Julie is thinking about her dead grandmother). There's no possible way that a film audience can discern either of these kinds of things from an actor's performance.

On the other hand, you can write what a character feels, if that's playable by an actor. As a screenwriter, though, you should never be guilty of "acting on paper." So as a rule, you should stay away from writing specific actions (he laughs, she wipes the sweat from her brow, he cocks an eyebrow) and instead concentrate on the underlying emotion (he's amused, she's nervous, he's puzzled). Not only does this allow an actor the freedom to practice his craft, but it also eliminates any confusion that may arise from the way that a specific physical action is presented in the script. If, for instance, you write a scene direction stating that a character shrugs, what's the reader to make of it? Is the character confused? Dejected? Indifferent? You want your readers reading your script, not attempting to decipher it.

An often-overlooked aspect of scene directions is the opportunity that they provide for introducing characters. The mechanics of character introduction are straightforward. A character's name is capitalized the first time he appears in the scene directions and only the first time. This alerts everyone involved in the production, including the actor playing the role, as to when a specific character enters the film. In your introduction of a character, include basic casting information such as age and gender, if the character's name does not make the latter clear. Also offer some sort of insight into the character with a brief line or two of description. This helps to provide the actor and the director (who may in fact be you) with a context for all the dramatic choices that are about to follow.

Be consistent in the way that you refer to your characters in scene directions. If a character's name is John, he should be identified by that name or by the appropriate pronoun throughout the screenplay. Don't worry about varying your prose with descriptive phrases substituted for a character's name. For example, keep away from scene directions like this:

```
John enters the room. The young man
crosses to the window, and there he
accidentally bangs his head into the
bottom of the window frame. The clumsy
man then turns back toward the center
of the room.
```

Reading these scene directions, someone breaking down a script for a shooting schedule might reasonably conclude that there are three different characters: John, the young man, and the clumsy man. The phrases "the young man" and "the clumsy man" would be better and more clearly written as the pronoun *he*.

In Focus: Character Introductions

How you introduce a character in the scene directions will go a long way toward shaping the way readers—including actors, designers, the producer, and the director—perceive him. Minor characters and non-speaking characters should receive no more than a word or two of introduction. But a protagonist and an antagonist deserve more. How much more is entirely up to you. Here are some possible approaches.

An Elaborate Introduction:

At the center of it all is WILLIAM "WILL" BARNES, IV, late 20s/early 30s. Despite the blue blazer and club tie he wears, despite the Bombay martini he sips, despite the fact that he looks like a refugee from an F. Scott Fitzgerald novel, there's something about him that puts him at odds with the very affluent, very white world around him.

A Less Elaborate Introduction:

DEEPHOUSE may be 30 or 35 or 40. It doesn't matter. No matter how many years he's lived, he's much older than that. And despite his good nature, you can detect a hint of loss and losing, an intimacy with defeat.

A Simple Introduction:

In the furniture store of life, ROB is a recliner.

Finally, leave plenty of white space on the pages of your screenplay. This will make it more readable as well as giving you a more accurate idea of the eventual running time of the finished film. A screenplay with page after page of densely written scene directions could turn out to be a film two to three times longer than the page count suggests. To avoid this possibility, make sure that paragraphs consist of no more than four or five lines of text. (That's not four of five *sentences*; that's four or five *lines*.) Once you reach the sixth line, it's time to start a new paragraph, even though that may seem contrary to everything you ever learned in English class.

Note

A good way to divide paragraphs in scene directions is to think of each new paragraph as a new shot. Of course, the screenplay won't actually indicate shots, but this mental picture will help you to keep your pages uncluttered and readable.

Character Cues

A character cue precedes dialogue and indicates which character will speak those particular lines. As in scene directions, consistency is absolutely crucial to the way characters are identified in character cues. If the character has a first name and a last name, you'll probably use just the first name. If you choose to use the last name instead, that's fine, too. But pick one and stick to it. Otherwise, confusion will arise over how many characters there are in your screenplay and just who speaks which lines.

Usually, a minor character with only a line or two of dialogue doesn't merit a proper name. Instead, you can use simple description to identify that character: bystander #1, bystander #2, drunken man, cop, delivery boy. It's important, though, that you refer to a character in the same way in scene directions as you do in character cues. And even though the character's name is capitalized in a character cue (for example, NUN #1), it's written entirely in lowercase in scene directions (nun #1). The only exception occurs when the character appears for the first time in the scene directions. As with any other character in that situation, the name is capitalized.

Dialogue

Write all the words that characters speak as dialogue. Don't paraphrase any of it in scene directions, even if lines are spoken by members of a group or a crowd. At the same time, don't write in dialogue what an actor will be playing. A character shouldn't have a line that reads, "I'm angry with you," when the actor can easily play anger and direct it at another character.

Parenthetical Directions

Parenthetical directions appear before a line of dialogue. These directions pertain specifically to the character speaking, and they almost always refer to the interpretation of the line that follows.

Parenthetical directions should be used with caution. Actors make their own choices about the way lines are read, so you should write a parenthetical direction only when the meaning of the line would otherwise be misunderstood. For example, if a character says, "I love you," but really means the opposite, you need to write a parenthetical direction suggesting that the line is either sarcastic or ironic.

You should never use a parenthetical direction simply to suggest the way you hear the line—for example, quietly, grim, or cracking up. Such directions are universally ignored by actors, which will just end up frustrating you.

Ideally, a parenthetical direction should be brief, consisting of no more than a word or two. Usually, that word is an adjective or an adverb. If, for some reason, a parenthetical direction extends longer than two lines of text, it should be reformatted and turned into a scene direction.

A parenthetical direction can also be used to indicate a special circumstance under which dialogue is spoken, such as voiceover narration, which is written as (v.o.), or off-camera dialogue, which is written as either (o.c.) or (o.s.).

In Focus: Off-camera Dialogue

Off-camera dialogue is spoken by someone physically present in a scene but unseen by the camera. It should be used sparingly in a screenplay because the blocking of the actors in relation to the camera is the responsibility of the director. Off-camera dialogue should not be confused with voiceover, which is dialogue that occurs outside the immediate on-screen world of the film. Voiceover is generally narration, and it's added to a film in post-production.

Transitions

In recent years, transitions (CUT TO, DISSOLVE TO) have fallen out of favor and have more or less disappeared from screenplays. The logic behind this is that nearly every transition from one scene to another is a cut, so why bother stating the obvious? And if, the reasoning continues, the transition is not a cut but a dissolve or something else, that choice is not the screenwriter's anyway.

While all this is true, there are instances when you may want to include transitions in your screenplay. If your script is nearly all scene directions with little or no dialogue, you would most likely add transitions to make the pages less dense with words as well as to give you a truer idea of the running time of your film.

In Focus: The Most Frequently Used Transitions

- CUT TO indicates a change in scenes without an optical transition.
- DISSOLVE TO indicates a change in which images from one scene are gradually replaced by images of another. Often DISSOLVE TO is used to suggest the passage of time without any real belief on the part of the screenwriter that an actual dissolve will be used in the final, edited film.
- FADE IN appears only at the beginning of the screenplay.
- FADE OUT appears only at the end of a screenplay.

The transition FADE TO BLACK tends to appear in films and screenplays more often than it really ought to. In this type of transition, the on-screen images are gradually replaced by black, and, once the screen is totally dark, it remains that way for a time. The problem is that filmmakers often use a fade simply as a way to get from one scene to another, when in fact it carries a very specific meaning in the language of film. By fading to black, a filmmaker calls attention to the scene that has just ended. With the audience seated in total darkness, he's implicitly instructing everyone to take a moment to consider the implications of that scene. The longer the period of darkness, the more contemplation the filmmaker expects of his audience.

The Standard Industry Format (Traditional)

The standard industry format has been in use almost since the beginning of film history in the United States. It sets forth with great specificity the way margins should be set and the use of appropriate capitalization and punctuation in screenplays.

(1)— <u>THEN AGAIN</u>

(2)— FADE IN:

(3)— EXT. AMTRAK STATION — 30TH STREET, PHILADELPHIA — DAY

(4)— A METROLINER lumbers into the station.

(5)— DISSOLVE TO:

INT. 30TH STREET STATION — STATION PLATFORM — DAY

Men and women dressed for business stream out of the Metroliner cars.

(6)——— DISPATCHER
(7)— (through the p.a. system)
(8)— This is the Metroliner from New York City arriving on track five. Metroliner from New York City. Continuing service to Wilmington, Baltimore, Washington....

(9)— After a moment, JAMES MACLEOD — late 30s, good-looking in a relaxed, seersucker way — straggles out of the train.

He pauses for a moment and looks around, as if he's half-expecting someone to greet him.

But all he sees is a mostly vacant platform and one or two trains, several tracks away, waiting to take on passengers.

CUT TO:

INT. 30TH STREET STATION — CONCOURSE — DAY

Riding an escalator from the station platform below, James slowly rises into the cavernous room as DEPARTURE
(10)— AND ARRIVAL ANNOUNCEMENTS echo murkily from the public address system.

He steps off the escalator, and, passing a trashcan, he
(11)— tosses in a MAGAZINE, some sort of college alumni publication.

On the open page, the headline reads, "ALUMNI TO BE HONORED IN JUNE."

CUT TO:

Figure 7.1 Traditional industry screenplay format (page 1).

⑫— 2.

EXT. 30TH STREET STATION — TAXI STAND — DAY

A TAXI pulls up.

James opens a back door and slides in.

                    JAMES
          University City.

                              CUT TO:

EXT. COLLEGE GREEN — DAY

Scattered sunbathers speckle the green.

A dog with a bandana tied around its neck catches a frisbee
on the fly.

Here and there, T-shirted students greet one other with the
boisterousness of long-anticipated farewells.

Men and women, who are from all appearances professors,
wander aimlessly out of a variety of CLASSROOM AND
ADMINISTRATION BUILDINGS.

                              CUT TO:

EXT. BROWNSTONE — UNIVERSITY CITY — DAY

The taxi pulls up, and James gets out.

He takes a long look around, as if he's not completely
certain that this is his destination.

                    CAB DRIVER
          Sure this is where you want to go?

                    JAMES
          Couldn't be surer.

He hands a ten-dollar bill to the driver.

                    JAMES
          Keep the change.

James now turns to face the building, a three-story three-
flat.

He abruptly sidesteps two burly students, who nearly level
him with the box spring they carry to a U-HAUL TRUCK.

He watches the students struggling with the box spring for
a moment and then starts up the steps.

Figure 7.2 Traditional industry screenplay format (page 2).

1. At the top of the first page, which is not numbered, the title is centered, capitalized, and underlined.

2. Double-spaced below and aligned to the left margin set at 1.75 inches is the transition "FADE IN."

3. Scene headings are aligned to the left margin and capitalized.

4. Scene directions are aligned to the left margin and written in upper and lowercase. A vehicle integral to the scene is capitalized the first time it's mentioned in the scene directions.

5. Transitions are capitalized and set at 4.25 inches from the left margin.

6. Character cues are set at 3.675 inches from the left margin and written entirely in capital letters.

7. Parenthetical directions are set at 2.125 from the left margin, written entirely in lowercase letters, and enclosed by parentheses.

8. Dialogue is set at 1.25 from the left margin.

9. When a character appears for the first time in the screenplay, his name is capitalized in the screen directions. After that, the character's name appears as it ordinarily would, capitalized if it's a proper name (James, Suzy, Chuckles), lowercase if it's a common noun (the thief, the homeless man, the yapping little dog).

10. Sound cues and special effects are capitalized.

11. A prop that's integral to the scene is capitalized the first time it appears in the directions for that scene.

12. Page numbering begins on page two. Numbers appear in the upper-right corner, and each is followed by a period.

The Standard Industry Format (Updated)

Over the years, the standard industry format has evolved. The changes, while not extreme, are worth noting. They have managed to streamline both the appearance and the actual writing of screenplays.

(1)— EXT. AMTRAK STATION — 30TH STREET, PHILADELPHIA — DAY

(2)— A Metroliner lumbers into the station.   (3)—

INT. 30TH STREET STATION — STATION PLATFORM — DAY

Men and women dressed for business stream out of the
Metroliner cars.

                         DISPATCHER
                   (through the p.a. system)
               This is the Metroliner from New York
               City arriving on track five.
               Metroliner from New York City.
               Continuing service to Wilmington,
               Baltimore, Washington....

After a moment, JAMES MACLEOD — late 30s, good-looking in a
relaxed, seersucker way — straggles out of the train.

He pauses for a moment and looks around, as if he's half-
expecting someone to greet him.

But all he sees is a mostly vacant platform and one or two
trains, several tracks away, waiting to take on passengers.

INT. 30TH STREET STATION — CONCOURSE — DAY

Riding an escalator from the station platform below, James
slowly rises into the cavernous room as departure and
(4)— arrival announcements echo murkily from the public address
system.

He steps off the escalator, and passing a trashcan, he
(5)— tosses in a magazine, some sort of college alumni
publication.

As he walks away, we HOLD on the headline on the open page:
"ALUMNI TO BE HONORED IN JUNE."

EXT. 30TH STREET STATION — TAXI STAND — DAY

A taxi pulls up.

James opens a back door and slides in.

Figure 7.3 Updated industry screenplay format.

1. The left margin is set at 1.5 inches. On the first page, the title and the transition "FADE IN" are not included. Instead, the screenplay begins with the scene heading for the first scene. As in the traditional industry format, this page is not numbered.
2. Vehicles are not capitalized.
3. Transitions are not used, although an additional blank line may be included between the end of one scene and the scene heading that follows it.
4. Sound cues are not capitalized.
5. Significant props are not capitalized.

Even with the changes that have occurred over time, there's no single right way to format a script. You can certainly combine elements from the traditional format and the updated format just as long as your screenplay shares the general overall look that all other screenplays have.

The Title Page

Every screenplay needs a title page, although most contain more information than is truly necessary.

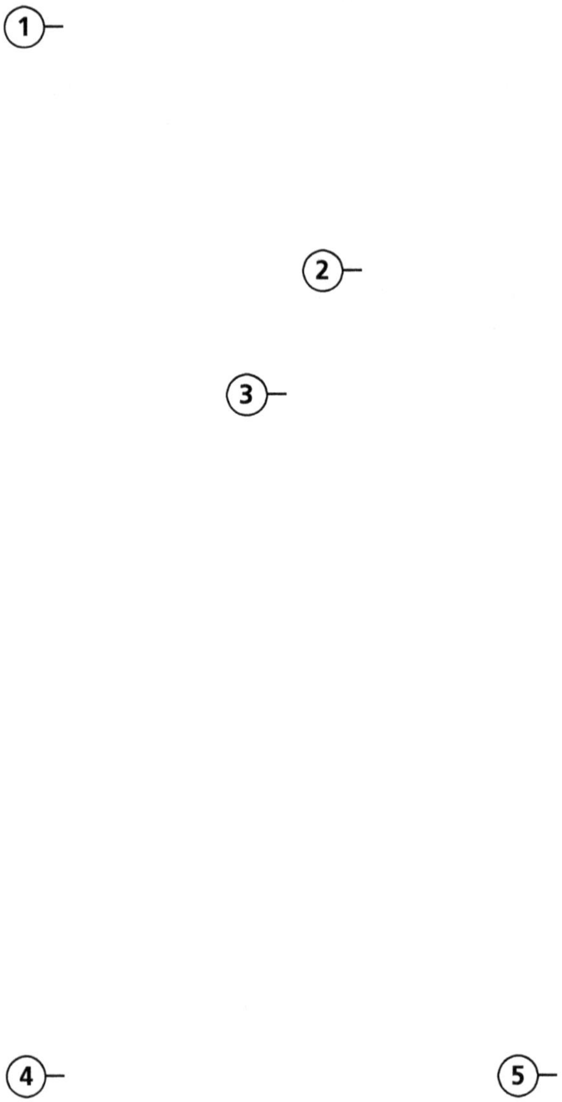

①—

②—

③—

④—   ⑤—

Figure 7.4 Title page.

1. Set the left margin on the title page to 1.5 or 1.75 inches. This provides a gutter so that no words are concealed when the script is bound. All other margins on the page are 1 inch.

2. Place the title about a third of the way down the page where it's centered and capitalized. Drop down another two lines. Using the shift key+hyphen key combination, create a solid line approximately the same width as the title.

3. Quadruple space (skip three lines), and then add information about the screenwriter(s).

4. Only date your screenplay once you're actively developing it for production and your collaborators need to know which draft they are reading.

5. If you're circulating your screenplay among people who don't know you, include contact information, which should be aligned to the right margin. Your work is protected by United States copyright law as soon as it is saved to your hard drive, so there's no need to include either a copyright notice or a Writers Guild registration notice.

Note

An alternative way to present title information is to type the word "by" on its own line, double-space, and then write the name(s) of the screenwriter(s). For example:

```
                    THEN  AGAIN
                  _____



                        by

                  Alan  Smithee
```

Special Situations

In the course of writing a screenplay, you may encounter situations that require special considerations in formatting. One of these is a telephone conversation.

If at all possible, you should avoid including phone conversations in your screenplay. The problem is that they are inherently non-dramatic. In theory, when two characters are in the same location, anything can happen. When two characters are on opposite ends of a telephone call, all they can do is talk. Always strive to create situations in which characters can come together in one location and actors can play the scene face to face.

Undoubtedly, there will come a time when you absolutely must write a telephone conversation (but write it *only* if you absolutely must). The first thing to do then is to decide the form of the conversation. Is it one-sided, two-sided with one character on-screen, or two-sided with two characters on-screen?

From a scheduling and production perspective, the easiest phone conversation to shoot is one-sided. In this sort of scene, an actor holds the phone to his ear and talks to an imaginary person who's neither seen nor heard. This requires the on-screen actor to pause every now and then, as if he's listening to what the imaginary person on the other end of the telephone line has to say.

On paper, a one-sided phone conversation might look like this:

```
                    WILL
               (on the phone)
     Hello....  Ginny, where are you...?
     Did you speak to your mother...?
     Listen, I think we should announce our
     engagement....
```

Notice two important characteristics of this kind of conversation. First, a parenthetical direction is used to indicate that the character is speaking into the telephone. Second, ellipsis points (...) are used to indicate those moments in the conversation when the on-screen character pauses to "listen" to the unseen and unheard character on the other end of the line.

A two-sided conversation in which only one character is on-screen is slightly more complicated than a one-sided conversation. Here, there are two main concerns: one, making sure that the on-screen actor allows enough time for the lines of the unseen actor to be spoken and, two, recording the lines of the unseen actor at some other time.

On paper, a two-sided phone conversation with one character on-screen might look like this:

```
INT. STUDY - NIGHT

A RINGING phone.  Will crosses to the desk to
answer it.

                    WILL
               (on the phone)

     Hello....
```

                         GINNY
                   (from the phone)
          Will ... it's so great to hear your
          voice.

                         WILL
          Ginny, where are you?

                         GINNY
          About a hundred miles south of Cairo.

                         WILL
          Did you speak to your mother?

                         GINNY
          She said you had something to tell me.

                         WILL
          Listen, I think we should announce our
          engagement.

                         GINNY
          Will, yes! The instant I get back.

Notice the important characteristics of this kind of conversation. First, a parenthetical direction is used to indicate that the first character is speaking into the phone. Next, a parenthetical direction is used to indicate that the other character is heard but not seen—that is, she's speaking "from the phone." Finally, once each character is established as speaking either on the phone or from the phone, the parenthetical directions stop.

In terms of performance and scheduling, the most demanding kind of telephone conversation is a two-sided conversation in which both sides are on-screen. Typically, each side of the conversation is shot in its entirety at its own location and then the two are edited together. Decisions about when an actor is seen speaking on camera and when his words are simply heard as the other character reacts to them are made in the editing suite. So as a screenwriter, you want to present the content of the telephone conversation as simply as possible.

On paper, a two-sided phone conversation with both characters on-screen might look like this:

INT. STUDY - NIGHT

A RINGING phone. Will crosses to the desk
to answer it.

                    WILL
              (on the phone)
    Hello....

EXT. BANKS OF THE NILE - ENCAMPMENT - DAY

As men in kaffiyehs break camp behind her,
Ginny holds the handset of a satellite-phone
to her ear.

                    GINNY
              (on the phone)
    Will....

TELEPHONE CONVERSATION - INTERCUT

between Will in the STUDY and Ginny
ALONG THE NILE.

                    GINNY
    It's so great to hear your voice.

                    WILL
    Ginny, where are you?

                    GINNY
    About a hundred miles south of Cairo.

                    WILL
    Did you speak to your mother?

                    GINNY
    She said you had something to tell me.

                    WILL
    Listen, I think we should announce our
    engagement.

                    GINNY
    Will, yes! The instant I get back.

Notice the differences between this two-sided conversation and the conversation that has only a single on-screen character.

1. A scene heading and scene directions establish each location.

2. A parenthetical direction indicates that each character is speaking on the phone.

3. Once this situation is established, the remainder of the conversation is presented as if it were just an ordinary scene, using the scene heading "PHONE CONVERSATION - INTERCUT" to introduce it.

4. The scene directions below this scene heading remind the reader in capital letters of the respective locations of the two characters.

5. The dialogue then plays out without any additional interruption in the exchanges.

Almost as common as telephone conversations are montages. Generally, a montage telescopes time (the change of seasons, the transition from day into night) or the development of a situation over time (a couple falling in love, a team struggling in a game).

Like telephone conversations, montages should be limited in their use, if not totally avoided. The issue is that, on paper, a montage looks deceptively easy to shoot. Everything appears under a single scene heading, and the whole thing takes up no more than one-quarter or one-third of a page.

Here's an example:

```
EXT. VERMONT COUNTRYSIDE - SERIES OF SHOTS -
DAY

The passenger train hurtles through country-
side, passing a series of vivid, rustic
tableaux....

In a quarry cut deep into the side of a
mountain, bare-chested men engage in the back-
breaking labor of cutting and hauling granite.

In a small, remote cemetery, a young widow and
her three children tend to a well-manicured
gravesite.

At a railroad crossing, in the front seat of
a Cadillac convertible, a dapper young man and
the beautiful flapper at his side eagerly doff
```

```
their hats at the passing train.

Eventually, on either side of the track
appear houses.  As the distance between them
narrows, a town begins to form.

Within moments, the train slows, and a rail-
road station comes into view.

The train slows to a steaming, hissing stop
in the station.
```

Can you see the problem with this montage? Under a single scene heading, there are at least seven locations, perhaps even more, depending on the way each paragraph of the script is shot. This means that a significant part of the shooting schedule will be devoted essentially to establishing a location. What's more, the time spent shooting this montage will be totally disproportionate to the screen time that results from it.

In the interest of streamlining a shooting schedule, you should always find an alternative to a montage. Selecting the entire montage in your word processing application and hitting the delete button is sometimes a possibility. If the information contained in the montage is absolutely crucial to the plot, coming up with a dramatic scene that actors can play is the best option.

Much less common than either montages or phone conversations is dual dialogue, which occurs when two characters speak simultaneously. Despite the fact that some well-known filmmakers have used overlapping dialogue to great effect, the truth is that there are very few situations in which dual dialogue is justified. Characters should be given the time to say what they need to say, and they should not have to compete with one another for the attention of the audience.

If there comes a time when you decide that this kind of dialogue is absolutely necessary, you would format it in this way:

```
    ACTOR #1              ACTOR #2
  Let me speak.    I have something to say.
```

Some Simple but Essential Rules of Punctuation

Although film grammar may be more important than English grammar in screenwriting, you must always write with precision and clarity to ensure that your ideas are totally understood by the people reading your screenplay. Nowhere is this more critical than in the use of punctuation, which can convey real subtleties, especially to your cast.

- Use a dash, which is usually typed as a hyphen, to indicate that dialogue spoken by one character is interrupted by another character.

                    ACTOR
    Just give me a new line, and I'll -

                 SCREENWRITER
    Not on your life.

Note

Be judicious in your use of incomplete lines of dialogue. Because an actor will continue to speak an incomplete line until he's interrupted by another actor, you may find your dialogue filled out in unexpected ways.

- Use a dash, typed as a hyphen, to indicate an abrupt change in attitude within a line of dialogue.

    If I just had a different line - hey,
    did I mention that you're an unbeliev-
    ably talented screenwriter?

- Use ellipsis points (...) to indicate a more gradual change in attitude within a line of dialogue.

    Rewriting is such a big ... well, it's
    a huge job.

- Use ellipsis points to indicate a less abrupt conclusion to incomplete dialogue, a situation in which a character does not finish his thought but is not interrupted at the end of his line.

    If I have to work with one more actor
    who wants to change my lines ...

■ Use ellipsis points to indicate that a character is listening to someone speak on the other end of a telephone conversation.

SCREENWRITER
(on the phone)

```
You like my script....  You're paying
me how much for it...?  No way...!
```

In Focus: Ellipsis

Notice that an ellipsis at the end of a complete statement includes a fourth period, which is, logically, the period that ends the sentence. An ellipsis in the form of a question requires three periods and a question mark—in that order. An ellipsis can also take the form of an exclamation with three periods and an exclamation point—in that order. Anytime an ellipsis uses four punctuation marks, it is placed flush against the last word in the sentence—that is, there's no space between the last word and the punctuation that follows it. Anytime an ellipsis requires just three periods, it's separated from the last word in the sentence by a space and separated from the first word in the next sentence by two spaces.

■ In dialogue, when one character addresses another by name, use commas to set off the name of the person addressed.

```
Charles Foster Kane, when are you
going to learn that empire-building
does not lead to peace of mind?
```

```
I hate to tell you this, Wolverine, but
you're in serious need of a manicure.
```

```
So what kind of batteries does this
light saber take, Obi?
```

■ Use commas to set off a character addressed, even if he isn't addressed by his proper name.

```
Buddy, can you spare a dime?
```

```
So, little guy, is it really true that
you see dead people?
```

```
Here's looking at you, kid.
```

- Use commas to separate an interjection from the rest of a sentence.

```
I'm not going, no.

Yes, you are!

Well, okay, let's go.
```

- Use commas to separate a filler phrase like "you know," "I mean," and "like" from the rest of a sentence.

```
You know, I was, like, going to the
mall. I mean, there were tons of
things on sale, you know.
```

- When you want to emphasize words in lines of dialogue, underline rather than italicize or capitalize. (But don't overdo it.)

```
I told you never to do that again.
```

Screenwriter's Notebook: Commonly Misspelled and Misused Words

Right	Wrong
all right	alright
okay, o.k., OK	ok, O. K.
yeah (pronounced "yeh")	yea (pronounced "yay")

The phrase *every day* is two words when referring to how often something happens, as in the sentence "I spend time every day working on my screenplay." *Everyday* is one word when describing something as common or usual, as in the sentence "Gaining insights into my characters is an everyday occurrence."

Chapter Seven, Take Two—Chapter Review

- By writing in the standard industry format, you accomplish two things:
  - You develop a reasonably good idea of the running time of the completed film based on your screenplay.
  - You allow readers to concentrate on the content of your screenplay and the strength of your ideas rather than the eccentricities of layout.

- Screenplays are written in the present tense, using master scenes.
- There are six main elements in a formatted screenplay:
  - Scene heading
  - Scene direction
  - Character cue
  - Parenthetical direction
  - Dialogue
  - Transition
- Be consistent in the way that you refer to your characters in scene directions and character cues.
- Limit the use of telephone conversations, which are inherently non-dramatic.
- Limit the use of montages, which take up a disproportionately large part of a shooting schedule but yield a relatively short amount of screen time.

Wrap

Several years ago, in a television commercial for a fitness product, a well-known singer-turned-actress proclaimed, "If having a great body was easy, everyone would have one." She then quickly abandoned her fitness program and underwent several years of very obvious plastic surgery.

If writing a great short screenplay were easy, everyone would have one. But it's not. And there's no plastic surgery in screenwriting, no cosmetic substitute for the real effort required to get your script into shape for production. Useful tips and good advice may make your work go faster and your finished script better. But the actual hands-on work can be done by only one person—you. And, once you're done writing, you're really just getting started. You need to assemble your production team, and then go out and make your movie.

Yes, it's a lot of work. A *lot* of work. So what are you waiting for?

Appendix A

Genres

Genres provide a method of classifying films according to characteristics that they have in common. Films that share similar styles, themes, or structural elements are considered in the same genre. Those specific settings, archetypal characters, story events, and values that recur in any given genre are called genre conventions.

So why are genres so important? The critic Jeffery Lyons has one of the best answers. "Audiences don't understand the genre," he has said. "The genre understands the audience." In other words, a genre doesn't create expectations so much as answer fundamental desires in an audience. People will go to see a film in a particular genre simply to have those desires fulfilled. This doesn't mean that you as a screenwriter can't experiment with genres. Some memorable films have come from the unexpected combination of genres. Before Mel Brooks, who would have thought that westerns (or horror or science fiction) could be hilarious? What's more, some genres, like war films and love stories, are almost always combined with at least one other genre.

While genres are enormously important in feature films—especially in commercial Hollywood films—they are less so in short films. For practical reasons, most short films are set in the present, they use little in the way of effects, and their brevity limits structural choices. As a result, screenwriters usually lack the screen time and the resources to incorporate those styles, themes, and plot devices that are the hallmarks of a genre. Still, you may find that the short film that you are writing is of a particular genre or at least shares some of its conventions. And, even if you don't, recognizing the major genres and their focus is critical to your development as a screenwriter and a filmmaker.

THE MAJOR GENRES

Genre	Focus	Common Sub-genres
action/adventure	feats of physical daring	*high adventure:* action informed by big themes of honor, duty, patriotism, and posterity; very often a period piece *disaster:* a man-made or natural disaster and its consequences
animation	anything other than live-action	*cel-painted* *computer-generated* *claymation* *interpolated rotoscoping* *stop motion*
biography	stories set in the past and focused on an individual rather than an era	
buddy movie	friends (existing or soon-to-be) coming together for the benefit of one or all	
cautionary drama	the dark side of human nature	*punishment story:* the good turn bad and pay the price *disillusionment story:* the protagonist's view of life, people, or himself changes from positive to negative
comedy	laughter from benign to caustic	*black:* the comic treatment of a serious subject like murder or nuclear holocaust *farce:* over-the-top comedy derived from improbable situations populated by stereotypical characters *mockumentary:* fake documentary *romantic:* love from a humorous perspective *parody:* comedy that comes from copying and mocking another film or work of art *satire:* an attack on vices and stupidity, usually of an institutional variety *screwball:* broad situational comedy in which women are shown to be superior to men while common working-class people are shown to be superior to wealthy, socially prominent individuals

Genre	Focus	Common Sub-genres
		slapstick: physical comedy, often featuring exaggerated but harmless violence
coming of age	a rites-of-passage film in which the protagonist grows and matures	frequently combined with comedy generally and romantic comedy specifically
crime	law-breaking in its many forms	sub-genres are distinguished by the protagonist who drives the action
		caper: professional criminal
		courtroom: lawyer
		detective: cop
		espionage: spy
		film noir: the protagonist is in part a criminal, a victim, and an amateur detective
		gangster: organized crime figure
		murder mystery: private detective
		newspaper/newsroom: journalist
		prison: inmate
		thriller: victim
docudrama	the recent past (ten to fifteen years) rather than the distant past	
fantasy	an unreal world free from the rules of time, space, and the physical universe	
historical drama	films set in the past but focused on the era rather than an individual	
horror	bizarre, frightening events	*rational:* subject to plausible explanation—anything from scientific experimentation gone awry to visiting extraterrestrials
		supernatural: the spirit world, including ghosts and their otherworldly variations
love story	the evolution of a romance	often combined with comedy

Genre	Focus	Common Sub-genres
musical	a stylized version of reality in which characters sing their thoughts and feelings (and sometimes dance as well)	
road movie/ road picture	a journey through exotic locations	
science fiction	a hypothetical future	
social drama	the dramatization of a problem in society	sub-genres are distinguished by the specific problem addressed in the film *domestic drama:* family problems *eco-drama:* environmental issues *medical drama:* illness *political drama:* politics, usually with a focus on corruption *woman's film:* problems of females in contemporary society
sports	athletics as narrative or metaphor	
test of will	the inner strength of the characters in the face of enormous adversity, which might range from climbing Mt. Everest to keeping a family farm in operation when big business threatens to take it over	
uplifting drama	feel-good films in which the protagonist triumphs	*education story:* the protagonist's view of life, people, or himself changes from negative to positive *redemption story:* the protagonist undergoes a moral change from bad to good
war	combat and its consequences, whether on the front lines or on the home front	
western	maintaining law and order in the Western frontier of the late 19th Century	

Appendix B

Glossary

A-plot The main plot in a film that has one or more subplots. Also known as *an action line* or *a foreground line.*

action The progressive dramatic movement of the plot.

action line See *A-plot.*

aerial shot A shot taken from an airplane or a helicopter.

allegory A type of film in which the characters and the plot stand for ideas larger than themselves.

angle The position of a camera in photographing a scene.

ANGLE ON A direction in a scene heading narrowing the focus of the scene to one part of the existing location.

antagonist The character that presents the main opposition to the protagonist as that character pursues his objective.

antihero A character that evokes audience identification even though he's not brave, noble, good, or otherwise heroic in nature. Antiheroes are typically outlaws or characters on the fringes of society.

arc The growth or change that a character undergoes during the course of the film's action. Sometimes referred to as a *character arc.*

art director The individual who oversees the design and construction of sets in a film production.

attitude The way that the world views a character.

audience identification The empathetic connection that an audience makes with a character or characters in a film.

backdrop The specific social environment in which a story takes place.

background line See *B-plot*.

back-story Significant events in the lives of the characters occurring prior to fade-in and affecting the central action as it unfolds. Also written as *back story* or *backstory*.

B-plot The main subplot in a film with one or more subplots. Also known as a *character line* or a *background line*.

beat A unit of action defined by the occurrence of a change. Beats can be divided into two categories: (1) major beats (also called story events) in which the change is so great that it moves the plot forward; (2) minor beats, which are the smaller changes that make up the underlying structure of any given scene.

beat sheet See *step outline*.

blocking Arranging the positions and movements of the actors and the camera in a scene.

body double A performer who takes the place of a featured actor in a scene that requires nudity or unusual physical fitness.

bridge scene A scene that provides a transition into a dramatic scene but has no dramatic purpose of its own. It's used to establish the time, the place, or the special circumstances of the dramatic scene that follows it.

buddy movie A film genre in which two friends (existing or soon-to-be) come together for the benefit of either or both.

button The inciting incident for a scene.

camera directions Directions concerning the movement of the camera as it follows the action or changes the view of the person, the object, or the scene being photographed. Examples are pan, tilt, zoom, and track. Camera directions are rarely, if ever, included in a screenplay.

catalyst A character whose sole purpose is to cause something to happen.

cause and effect The principle that an action or an event will produce a response in the form of another event.

central action The main progressive dramatic movement of the plot.

character arc See *arc.*

character line See *B-plot.*

characters The fictional figures that inhabit the world of a film.

chase A scene or a sequence involving the physical pursuit of characters or objects.

cinematographer An individual with expertise in capturing moving images through the use of cameras and lighting. The chief cinematographer in a production is called the director of photography.

clearance Express permission given by the owner of copyright-protected or trademark-protected material for its inclusion in a film.

cliché An overused plot device, story concept, or storytelling technique.

climax The last and highest dramatic moment in the rising action.

close-up A shot that provides a magnified view of a character or an object.

closed ending An ending that both resolves the conflict and brings a conclusive end to the plot.

composition The use of light, space, movement, and camera angle within the framed image.

concept The story for a screenplay expressed in a single sentence that identifies the protagonist, the protagonist's objective, and the obstacle that stands in the way of realizing it. Compare with *logline.*

condition lock A requirement that must be met for an objective to be realized or for a conflict to be resolved. Typically, the requirement can be summarized in an if-then statement.

confidant A character whose sole purpose is to allow another character to reveal himself by speaking his mind or otherwise externalizing his feelings.

conflict The fundamental opposition between characters or between a character and a dramatic force (nature, society, fate).

continuity Consistency in the details of a scene—makeup, wardrobe, lighting, set dressing, special effects—that allows different takes to be cut together to provide the illusion of continuous action.

credits The on-screen list of production personnel, including actors. Credits are often shown at both the beginning of a film (opening credits) and the conclusion (closing credits).

crisis A point in the action in which a character encounters an obstacle.

crosscutting The technique of interweaving the action from two or more scenes to indicate simultaneous action.

cut A change of shots without an optical transition.

CUT TO A transitional element that may be included at the end of the scene in a screenplay. Once used in all screenplays, it is now less common, replaced instead by a blank line.

denouement See *resolution.*

description See *scene directions.*

dialogue The words that the characters speak.

director The individual who is the principal creative force in the production of a film. The director's varied responsibilities include script development, casting, directing the cast, directing the crew, supervising post-production, and collaborating with the producer on financial and logistical matters.

director of photography The individual responsible for the artistic and technical quality of the photographed images in a production.

dissolve An editing technique in which the images from one shot are gradually replaced with the images of another. Also known as a *lap dissolve.*

DISSOLVE TO A transitional element that may be included at the end of a scene in a screenplay, often to suggest the passage of time.

dramatic action See *action.*

dramatic irony A narrative strategy in which the audience knows more than the characters about what is taking place on-screen.

drive-up A scene in which a vehicle arrives at a location, often for no real dramatic purpose.

editor The individual who performs the visual editing of a film in consultation with the director.

empathy Understanding a character's feelings and being moved by that understanding.

episodic Lacking a clear cause and effect between scenes or dramatic moments.

establishing shot   A shot that establishes the location of a scene. Traditionally, this has been a wide-angle view, but in recent years directors and cinematographers have become much more inventive in the way that they establish locations.

exchange The back-and-forth speaking of dialogue between characters.

exposition A narrative device providing information not evident from the events on the screen but necessary to the audience's understanding of the story.

EXT. In a scene heading, the indication that the following scene takes place outdoors (an exterior location).

extra A non-specific, non-speaking performer, typically appearing in the background of a scene or as part of a crowd.

FADE IN A transitional element in the first line of the screenplay, suggesting the use of a fade-in in the finished film.

fade-in A gradual on-screen transition from total blackness to an established image, occurring at the beginning of a film.

FADE OUT A transitional element in the last line of a screenplay, suggesting the use of a fade-out in the finished film.

fade-out A gradual on-screen transition from an established image to total blackness, occurring at the end of a film.

fade to black or **fade** A gradual on-screen transition from a normal image to total blackness, used either to point up the importance of the event that immediately precedes it or to suggest a sense of finality.

FADE TO BLACK A transitional element in the screenplay, suggesting the use of a fade in the finished film.

falling action See *resolution*.

feature film Historically, any film that runs 61 minutes or longer. In practice, feature-length films usually run at least 90 minutes, and many run much longer.

flashback An interruption in the present time of the action with a scene that takes place at an earlier point in the story. This device may be used for clarification or revelation, but it should never be used for simple exposition.

flashforward An interruption in the present time of the action with a scene that takes place at a future point in the story.

foreground line See *A-plot.*

genre A method to classify films according to stylistic, thematic, and/or structural elements that they have in common.

genre conventions The stylistic, thematic, and structural similarities of films in the same genre.

high-angle shot A shot that looks down on a scene, which is photographed from above.

image Photographed material as it appears on the screen.

inciting incident The event that sets the plot into full motion. It may occur either by the design of a character or by chance.

internal conflict A form of conflict pitting a character's objective against his need.

INT. In a scene heading, the indication that the following scene takes place indoors (an interior location).

into frame A technique in which the camera remains stationary and the subject walks into the shot.

into view A technique in which the camera moves to bring the subject of the shot into frame, while that subject remains stationary.

jump cut The editing together of two non-continuous shots within a scene.

lap dissolve See *dissolve.*

line-reading The way that a line of dialogue is performed by an actor.

live-action film A film shot with real people or animals on-screen.

logline A one- or two-line summary of the plot of a film. Compare with *concept.*

low-angle shot A shot that looks up at a scene, which is photographed from a position below eye level.

major beat See *beat.*

major dramatic question The central problem of the screenplay expressed in the form of a question.

master scene A written scene that includes scene directions and dialogue but excludes shots and camera movements.

medium shot A shot that falls between a close-up and a long shot in its field of view. In terms of a person, a view from the head to the hips might fill the frame in a medium shot.

minor beat See *beat.*

minor dramatic question The problem of the B-plot expressed in the form of a question.

monologue A long speech by a single actor.

montage Although there are many forms of montage, the term is most commonly used to describe a technique in which a series of shots are edited together to suggest in a short period of time the essence of events occurring over a longer period of time.

mystery A narrative strategy in which the audience knows less than the characters about what is taking place on-screen.

narrative The process of a telling a story.

naturalistic Imitating reality in an exact and faithful way.

need A character's subconscious desire or unacknowledged emotional want.

objective The goal that motivates a character's choices and actions. Objectives can be divided into two categories: (1) super-objective, which drives a character's actions throughout the entire film; (2) scene-objective, which drives a character's actions in a particular scene. A scene-objective should reflect either the character's super-objective or his need.

obligatory scene A scene implicitly promised to the audience through developments in the plot or the nature of the characters. The climax is almost always an obligatory scene because in traditional film narrative a conflict demands a resolution.

obstacle An emotional, intellectual, or physical hurdle that a character must overcome.

o.c. or **OC** A parenthetical direction indicating dialogue is spoken off-camera.

off-camera Someone or something physically present in a scene but unseen by the camera.

off-screen See *off-camera.*

open ending A climax that leaves the conflict partially or entirely unresolved and the plot without a definite conclusion.

o.s. or **OS** A parenthetical direction indicating dialogue is spoken off-screen.

outline A four- to seven-page prose summary of the plot of the film.

outlook The way a character views the world.

pan The action of moving a camera horizontally while remaining on a fixed base, either a tripod or a camera operator standing in one place.

parenthetical direction A direction that appears in parentheses prior to a line of dialogue in the script and suggests the way that line should be delivered. A parenthetical direction should be used only if the sense of the line written on the page would not be understood without it.

parody Any work of art that copies another work of art in a deliberate, comic, and satirical way.

period piece A film taking place in a time other than the present.

plant and payoff A preparatory device that presents information to an audience in a natural and understated manner so that it can be used to greater dramatic effect later in the action.

plot The choice of events that are dramatized on-screen and the order in which they are presented.

plural antagonist Two or more characters functioning as a single antagonist in pursuit of the same objective throughout the course of the action.

plural protagonist Two or more characters functioning as a single protagonist, working together in pursuit of the same objective throughout the course of the action.

point of attack The point in the story at which a scene or a screenplay begins.

point of view A camera angle that suggests the subjective perspective of a character in a scene.

post-production Work done on a film once it has been shot. This includes visual editing and sound editing.

POV See *point of view*.

premise The dramatic situation from which the conflict arises and the action unfolds.

preproduction The planning stage in the filmmaking process, a time when locations are scouted, sets are constructed, schedules and budgets are created, and the script is fine-tuned.

principal photography The stage of the filmmaking process in which a film is shot. Often referred to simply as *production*.

production designer The individual responsible for the design of the overall look of a film.

producer The individual who supervises the logistics of a production, including raising funds, hiring key personnel, and overseeing the budget and schedule (in collaboration with the director).

production draft The final draft of a screenplay written before a film goes into production.

production values A film's level of polish, determined by the quality of the image and sound, the elaborateness of the production design, the use of visual and special effects, and the degree of accomplishment in such craft areas as continuity and the blocking of extras.

proscenium The wall that separates the stage from the auditorium in a theater used for live performances.

protagonist The character whose super-objective drives the action of the film.

public domain The body of creative works and inventions to which no person or entity has any claim of legal ownership.

red herring A device that misdirects or misleads the audience into making false assumptions about the characters or the plot. Often used in detective stories, thrillers, and other plot-driven films dependent upon surprise.

resolution The screenplay's third and final structural part, centered on concluding the action and resolving the conflict.

revelation The dramatic disclosure of information that furthers the plot.

reversal A change so extreme that it causes the plot to reverse itself and move in an entirely different direction.

rising action A screenplay's main structural part consisting of a variety of escalating struggles that culminate in the climax.

running time The length of a finished film, measured in minutes, from opening credits through closing credits.

scene A unit of dramatic action characterized by the unity of time and the proximity of space.

scene-antagonist The character that provides the main opposition to the scene-protagonist as that character pursues his scene-objective.

scene directions The description of characters, locations, and physical action found in a screenplay. Sometimes referred to as *action, stage directions,* or *description.*

scene heading The element of the formatted screenplay that indicates the location of the scene and the time of day that it takes place. Sometimes referred to as a *slug line.*

scene-objective The goal that motivates a character's choices and actions in a scene. It should reflect some aspect of the character's super-objective or need. Compare with *super-objective.*

scene outline An outline for a screenplay in which each scene is broken down into minor beats. Compare with *step outline.*

scene-protagonist The character whose scene-objective drives the action in a scene.

scenery chewing Slang for an overly dramatic acting performance, especially one that comes off as overacting.

script supervisor In the production of a film, the individual who holds the shooting script and makes detailed notes about costumes, props, actors' appearances, etc., so that different takes match in the editing process.

sequence A series of scenes connected by a single idea.

setting The time and place of the story.

setup A screenplay's first structural part centered on establishing critical elements: setting, protagonist, tone, direction of the plot.

shooting script The script from which a film is shot.

shot list Developed by the director, a list that indicates the scenes scheduled for a shooting day. Usually included in each entry are the scene number, the location, a short description of the scene, the length of the scene in pages, a list of actors in the scene, and notes to departments of any special needs.

sides Script pages for a particular scene, often distributed on five-and-a-half by eight-inch paper so that an actor or a director can hold them comfortably in one hand while rehearsing or blocking.

slug line See *scene heading*.

smash cut A cut from one shot (or scene) to the next in a startlingly abrupt and obvious way. It can be suggested in the screenplay with the transitional direction SMASH CUT TO.

soliloquy A monologue intended to give the impression of unspoken musings. It is sometimes referred to as an *interior monologue*. Soliloquies are rarely, if ever, used in films.

sound editor The individual who edits the audio components of a film.

special effects Those effects—rain, snow, explosions, firearms hits—created live on the set.

squib A blood pack taped to a small explosive charge, which sits atop a padded plate that protects the actor wearing it. A remote triggering device fires the squib, spraying a blood-like substance.

stage directions See *scene directions*.

step outline A scene-by-scene outline of the major beats in the screenplay and the locations where those scenes take place. Also known as a *beat sheet*. Compare with *scene outline*.

story All the underlying events of the screenplay awaiting presentation by the screenwriter. This includes even those events occurring prior to fade-in, following fade-out, and taking place off-screen (events the screenwriter eventually chooses not to dramatize).

story event See *beat*.

structure All the constructed on-screen narrative, including the major and minor beats in every scene.

stunt double A stunt performer who assumes the role of a cast member in the performance of a stunt.

subplot A secondary plot that complements the main plot.

subtext The underlying, unspoken meaning of a line of dialogue, a speech, or a scene.

super-objective The goal that drives a character's choices and actions throughout the entire film. Compare with *scene-objective*.

suspense A narrative strategy in which the audience possesses the same information as the characters about what is taking place on-screen.

suspension of disbelief The ability of an audience to repress the knowledge that a film or a play is an invention and to respond to dramatic events as if they are real.

sympathy Experiencing feelings identical to those of a character on-screen.

synch sound The simultaneous use of images and their corresponding sounds as they seem to occur in real life. The full term is *synchronous sound*.

synopsis A concise version of the screenplay's story told in three to five paragraphs.

take A single continuous recorded performance.

theme The ultimate meaning of a work derived from the characters, the actions that they take, and the consequences of those actions.

tilt The action of moving a camera either up or down.

time lock A deadline by which something must be accomplished for an objective to be realized or for a conflict to be resolved.

tracking shot A shot in which the camera and its mount are moved as it follows the subject recorded.

treatment Historically, a 20-50 page prose version of the story for a feature-length screenplay. Over time, it has come to mean any prose version of the story for a screenplay of any length.

unity of opposites A conflict in which a protagonist and an antagonist pursue objectives that are diametrically opposed to each other.

verisimilitude The appearance of being real or true.

visual effects Effects created in post-production by manipulating the recorded image.

v.o. Voiceover.

voiceover Narration, usually added in post-production, that occurs outside the immediate on-screen world of the film.

walk-and-talk A dialogue-intensive scene in which the characters walk as they speak and the camera moves with them. The walking distracts from the fact that the scene is really about two characters talking.

zoom To change the angle of view from a longer shot to a shorter shot—or vice versa—by adjusting the lens rather than moving the camera.

Appendix C

Sample Screenplay: Early Draft

I'M NO STUD

———

by
Randall Ehrmann

January 26, 2006

Alligator Productions
2900 Bedford Avenue
Brooklyn NY 11210
(718) 555-1212

EXT. BASKINGS HOME - NIGHT

The wind bullies an old sycamore. Leaves RUSTLE and heavy
branches CREAK. Moonlight breaks through the swaying
timber and alights upon a large and impressive country
home.

It's late enough that most should be asleep; however, light
from a second-story window suggests otherwise.

INT. BASKINGS HOME - MASTER BEDROOM - NIGHT

In the background, we hear the faint sounds of SENSUAL
pleasure.

Framed photographs on night stands and dressers chronicle
the life of STEPHEN BASKINGS, his wife CHERYL, their two
daughters, KRISTIN and CARRIE-ANN, and their dog, CLIPPER.

ANGLE ON THE BED

Toes twitch and turn underneath cotton covers as muted
WHIMPERS and MOANS tease the air.

We travel slowly up and over the bumps and curves of a
sheeted figure to reveal ...

STEPHEN, early 50s, lying motionless on his back, staring
blankly at the ceiling. One might wonder if he were dead
if it weren't for the occasional furrowed brow and flash of
inner torment from his eyes.

At his side is CHERYL, an attractive, relaxed woman in her
late 40s. She is propped against a padded headboard
reading a racy romance novel.

More HUSHED PLEASURES pervade ...

Distant WHIMPERS now finding a distinct rhythm.

                         STEPHEN
             Oh, this is great!

                         CHERYL
                  (committed to her novel)
             Put your headphones on.

                         STEPHEN
             Three nights in a row.

A LUSTFUL GROAN is heard in the distance. It takes its
time tormenting Stephen.

2.

                         STEPHEN
          I can't even tell who is who.

Cheryl looks up from her novel. Listens.

                         CHERYL
          Carrie-Ann.

                         STEPHEN
          She's not even married yet.

                         CHERYL
          She will be Sunday.

                         STEPHEN
          Why can't they get hotel rooms like
          normal people? I said I'd pay for it.

                         CHERYL
          Because they adore you, stupid. They
          want to be near you.
                    (snuggling up next to him)
          They want you to fry 'em bacon, and
          squeeze oranges, and cook em
          disgusting, runny eggs just like you
          did every weekend for 20 years.

                         STEPHEN
                    (beat)
          My eggs aren't runny.

Stephen turns, puts headphones on, pushes play on the Ipod.
A tinny, trebly BACH SONATA plays from the phones.

INT. CARRIE-ANN'S ROOM - NIGHT

Soft light spills from a closet, its door left ajar. A
wedding gown hangs center rung.

Carrie-Ann, early 20s, gorgeous, with gentle eyes and an
athletic body, is in bed and on top of WALTER, 20s, goofy
but attractive in his own way.

A tempered lust radiates between them.

INT. MASTER BEDROOM - NIGHT

Stephen appears to have fallen asleep, until ...

his eyes open wide to the harmonic WHIMPERS resonating from
Kristin's room.

3.

INT. KRISTIN'S ROOM - NIGHT

Moonlight rushes in through half drawn blinds revealing an
office/guest room. This used to be Kristin's bedroom.

Kristin, late 20s, beautiful, but in a natural, unassuming
way, lies in bed tossing her head side-to-side, WHIMPERING
as MIKE, late 20s and corporate good looking, works his
magic.

INT. MASTER BEDROOM - NIGHT

Stephen sits up abruptly, headphones still on.

                         STEPHEN
                    (loudly)
               Migraine happening, Cheryl.

                         CHERYL
               It will be over soon.

                         STEPHEN
               This can't be good for me. My psyche.

                         CHERYL
               You encouraged them to live "a
               passionate life, not to settle, never
               apologize."

We hear louder, more intense MOANING and GROANING in the
distance.

                         STEPHEN
               Jesus Christ, what are these guys
               trained studs or something?

Cheryl looks up from her book, smiles.

A brief beat.

She puts the book on the nightstand, moves closer to
Stephen, then tenderly removes the headphones from his
ears.

                         CHERYL
                    (whispering)
               You know what? You're a stud.

She nuzzles Stephen's ear.

                         STEPHEN
                    (dejected)
               I'm no stud.

4.

He slides down to his pillow.

More MOANS from the girls' bedrooms as Cheryl continues her seduction. A crooked smile from Stephen.

Still more MOANS in the background as ...

Cheryl kisses her way down Stephen's neck.

Even more muffled GRUNTS and GROANS, until suddenly -

Stephen tosses the covers aside and bolts upright.

>   STEPHEN
>   That's it! The girls are sleeping in
>   here with us.

>   CHERYL
>   You're crazy, silly man. Lie down.

>   STEPHEN
>   I'll drag 'em in here by their
>   ponytails if I have to.
>   (fumbling with slippers)
>   I can take those geeky husbands of
>   theirs any day. Both of em' at the
>   same time, even.

Cheryl's played nicey nice long enough. She grabs Stephen by his pajama top, throws him back into bed. The shirt rips.

>   CHERYL
>   Lie down and shut up. Want to ruin
>   the most important weekend of your
>   daughter's life?

Stephen attempts escape - some MOANING and GROANING of his own - but Cheryl has him pinned down.

He continues squirming and thrusting violently - the headboard SLAMMING against the wall - loudly, rhythmically.

INT. KRISTIN'S ROOM - NIGHT

Mike and Kristin pause in their erotic endeavors. They listen to what sounds suspiciously like sexual activity coming from their parent's bedroom.

INT. CARRIE-ANN'S ROOM - NIGHT

Carrie-Ann and Walter also stop their intermingling and look at each other in disbelief.

5.

INT. MASTER BEDROOM - NIGHT

Stephen breaks free and bolts for the door.

Cheryl leaps from the bed and tackles him to the floor.

INT. CARRIE-ANN'S ROOM - NIGHT

We hear the loud THUMP from Stephen and Cheryl's room,
followed by a series of GIGGLES and muffled conversation.

Carrie-Ann is impressed. She smiles big.

But the parental excitement has the opposite effect on
Walter. She scrambles to regain his attention.

INT. MASTER BEDROOM - NIGHT

Stephen is face down, crawling on his belly toward the
door.

Cheryl has him by the ankles, dragging him backwards.

                    CHERYL
          God Damn it!

She drops to the floor and starts tickling him. Stephen
can't take it, lets out a series of short, GRUNT like
giggles.

                    CHERYL
          Are you going to stop?

                    STEPHEN
          No.

She takes it up a notch. More tickles, pinches and pokes.

                    STEPHEN
          No. No. No.

                    CHERYL
                (loudly)
          Yes. Yes. Yes.

INT. KRISTIN'S ROOM - NIGHT

Kristin and Mike lie on their backs staring out ... libidos
long gone.

                    MIKE
          Gonna be a real nice wedding.

6.

                                    KRISTIN
              Should be.

                                    MIKE
              Did you pack my navy blue socks?

INT. CARRIE-ANN'S ROOM - NIGHT

Walter has found the courage to continue on, but ...

                                    CARRIE-ANN
              I love you, baby.

No response.

                                    CARRIE-ANN
              Hello?

                                    WALTER
              Sorry.

Another MOAN is heard from the adjoining bedroom.

                                    WALTER
              I love you too.

INT. MASTER BEDROOM - NIGHT

Through great effort, Stephen has made his way to the door.

He hangs on the doorknob - half his body bent under Cheryl.

He turns and jiggles the handle desperately.

                                    CHERYL
              Don't! Stop! I swear to God, if you
              turn that handle one more time I'll
              take a chunk right out of your ass.

Stephen pauses a moment, considering.

                                    STEPHEN
              You're bluffing.

He turns the handle, starts to open door.

Cheryl instantly sinks her canines into Stephen's fleshy
ass. She GROWLS and GROANS orgasmically.

Pure disbelief, coupled with tremendous pain, registers on
Stephen's contorted face.

                                    STEPHEN
              Oh, Dear, God, All, Mighty!

7.

SERIES OF SHOTS: STEPHEN'S "MIGHTY" MOMENT ECHOING
THROUGHOUT

A) Empty kitchen.

B) Empty living room.

C) Empty hallway.

D) Doghouse: CLIPPER covers his eyes and ears with paws.

INT. CARRIE-ANN'S ROOM - NIGHT

Silence.

Carrie-Ann and Walter lie with their backs to each other,
pillows folded around their heads - Walter with an
intrigued, then contemplative expression.

INT. KRISTIN'S ROOM - NIGHT

Kristin and Mike are hidden underneath the covers.

Beat.

                    MIKE
          I gotta take a leak.

INT. MASTER BEDROOM - NIGHT

Stephen rubs his wound, his back to Cheryl, who sits on the
floor trying desperately not to laugh.

A big exhale, then Stephen turns the doorknob.

                    CHERYL
          Stephen, please? Don't?

Another beat before he turns to her, smiles amiably.

                    STEPHEN
          Just need to grab an ice pack for my
          ass, sweetie. I'll be right back.

Cheryl smiles sheepishly as Stephen turns to go.

INT. HALLWAY OFF MASTER BEDROOM - NIGHT

Stephen, in ripped and torn pajamas, closes the door behind
him and limps down the hallway.

8.

ANGLE ON KRISTIN'S DOOR

Mike comes out of Kristin's bedroom, spots Stephen, does an
immediate 180 but then pauses, decides to forge ahead.

They share an awkward moment in passing. A few steps more
until they both turn and look over their shoulders.

Mike nods in recognition of Stephen's talent.

Stephen's confused, but half-smiles anyway, rubbing his
ass.

                    STEPHEN
          Need some ice.

Mike just nods and shrugs as if to say, "Of course, who
wouldn't," and then crosses into the bathroom.

Stephen continues on, then glances back once more, puzzled.

ANGLE ON CARRIE-ANN'S DOOR

The sound of a DOOR unlatching and opening. Out pops
Walter's head, then the rest of his body when he confirms
it's Stephen.

He signals for Stephen to approach.

An awkward beat as they both just stand there in silence.

                    WALTER
          Mr. Baskings, I know this is terribly
          inappropriate and doubly embarrassing,
          but I just wanted to say ... thank
          you.

Stephen raises an eyebrow, awaits more information.

                    WALTER
          I, ah, I hope 20 years from now Carrie-
          Ann and I are as passionate for each
          other as you and Mrs. Baskings are.

A confused beat ... lingering until suddenly a big, bright,
blinding light switches on in Stephen's brain. He starts
to correct the misunderstanding, but -

                    WALTER
          You inspire me, Sir.
                    (pause)
          Bravo.

9.

INT. CARRIE-ANN'S ROOM - NIGHT

Carrie-Ann can't believe it. She rolls her eyes and
retreats further under cover.

INT. HALLWAY - CARRIE-ANN'S DOOR - NIGHT

Stephen takes a moment. Looks back toward his closed
bedroom door, smiles and turns back to Walter.

He gives Walter's shoulder a squeeze, nods and then
continues on toward the kitchen, rubbing his wounded ass.

The sound of a DOOR gently closing.

                                        FADE OUT.

Appendix
D

Sample Screenplay: Shooting Script

I'M NO STUD

———————

by
Randall Ehrmann

REVISED - March 26, 2006
(BLUE)

Alligator Productions
2900 Bedford Avenue
Brooklyn NY 11210
(718) 555-1212

EXT. BASKINGS HOME - NIGHT   1

The wind bullies an old sycamore. Leaves RUSTLE and heavy
branches CREAK. Moonlight breaks through the swaying
timber and alights upon a large and impressive country
home.

It's late enough that most should be asleep; however, light
from a second-story window suggests otherwise.

INT. BASKINGS HOME - MASTER BEDROOM - NIGHT   2 *

In the background, we hear the faint sounds of SENSUAL
pleasure.

Framed photographs on night stands and dressers chronicle
the life of STEPHEN BASKINGS, his wife CHERYL, their two
daughters, KRISTIN and CARRIE-ANN, and their dog, Clipper.

ANGLE ON THE BED   3 *

Toes twitch and turn underneath cotton covers as muted
WHIMPERS and MOANS tease the air.

We travel slowly up and over the bumps and curves of a
sheeted figure to reveal ...   *

STEPHEN, early 50s, lying motionless on his back, staring   *
blankly at the ceiling. One might wonder if he were dead
if it weren't for the occasional furrowed brow and flash of
inner torment from his eyes.

At his side is CHERYL, an attractive, relaxed woman in her   *
late 40s. She is propped against a padded headboard
reading a racy romance novel.

More HUSHED PLEASURES pervade ...   *

Distant WHIMPERS now finding a distinct rhythm.

                        STEPHEN
              Oh, this is great!

                        CHERYL
                 (committed to her novel)
              Put your headphones on.

                        STEPHEN
              Three nights in a row.

                                          (CONTINUED)

REVISED - 3/29/06 (Blue)   2.

3   CONTINUED: 3

A LUSTFUL GROAN is heard in the distance. It takes its
time tormenting Stephen.

                    STEPHEN
          Hard to tell who is who.   *

Cheryl looks up from her novel. Listens.

                    CHERYL
          Carrie-Ann.

                    STEPHEN
          She's not even married yet.

                    CHERYL
          She will be Sunday.

                    STEPHEN
          Why can't they get hotel rooms like
          normal people? I said I'd pay for it.

                    CHERYL
          Because they adore you, stupid. They
          want to be near you.
                    (snuggling up next to him)
          They want you to fry 'em bacon, and   *
          squeeze oranges, and cook 'em   *
          disgusting, runny eggs just like you
          did every weekend for 20 years.

                    STEPHEN
                    (beat)
          My eggs aren't runny.

Stephen turns, puts headphones on, pushes play on the Ipod.
A tinny, trebly BACH SONATA plays from the phones.

4   INT. CARRIE-ANN'S ROOM - NIGHT   4

Soft light spills from a closet, its door left ajar. A
wedding gown hangs center rung.

Carrie-Ann, early 20s, gorgeous, with gentle eyes and an   *
athletic body, is in bed and on top of WALTER, 20s, goofy   *
but attractive in his own way.

A tempered lust radiates between them.

5   INT. MASTER BEDROOM - NIGHT   5 *

Stephen appears to have fallen asleep, until ...   *

                                              (CONTINUED)

REVISED - 3/29/06 (Blue)　　　　　3.

5　CONTINUED:　　　　　　　　　　　　　　　　　　　　5

His eyes open wide to the harmonic WHIMPERS resonating from
Kristin's room.

6　INT. KRISTIN'S ROOM - NIGHT　　　　　　　　　　6

Moonlight rushes in through half drawn blinds revealing an
office/guest room.

Kristin, late 20s, beautiful, but in a natural, unassuming　　*
way, lies in bed tossing her head side-to-side, WHIMPERING
as MIKE, late 20s and corporate good looking, works his　　*
magic.

7　INT. MASTER BEDROOM - BED - NIGHT　　　　　　　7*

Stephen sits up abruptly, headphones still on.

　　　　　　　　　STEPHEN
　　　Migraine happening, Cheryl.　　　　　　　　*

　　　　　　　　　CHERYL
　　　It will be over soon.

　　　　　　　　　STEPHEN
　　　This can't be good for me.　　　　　　　　*

　　　　　　　　　CHERYL　　　　　　　　　　*
　　　You encouraged them to live a　　　　　　*
　　　passionate life, "never settle, never　　*
　　　apologize."　　　　　　　　　　　　　*

We hear louder, more intense MOANING and GROANING in the
distance.

　　　　　　　　　CHERYL
　　　A couple of studs.　　　　　　　　　　*

Stephen flashes Cheryl a look.　　　　　　　　　*

A brief beat and then she puts the book on the nightstand,　*
moves closer to Stephen, then tenderly removes the　　　　*
headphones from his ears.　　　　　　　　　　　*

　　　　　　　　　CHERYL　　　　　　　　　　*
　　　You know what?　You're my stud.　　　　　*

She nuzzles Stephen's ear.　　　　　　　　　　*

　　　　　　　　　STEPHEN　　　　　　　　　*
　　　I'm no stud.　　　　　　　　　　　　*

　　　　　　　　　　　　　　　(CONTINUED)

REVISED - 3/29/06 (Blue)   4.
7   CONTINUED: 7

He slides down to his pillow.   *

More MOANS from the girls' bedrooms as Cheryl continues her
seduction. A crooked smile from Stephen.

Still more MOANS in the background as ...   *

Cheryl kisses her way down Stephen's neck.

Even more muffled GRUNTS and GROANS, until suddenly -   *

Stephen tosses the covers aside and bolts upright.

                         STEPHEN
               That's it! The girls are sleeping in
               here with us.

                         CHERYL
               You're crazy, honey. Lie down.   *

                         STEPHEN
               I'll drag 'em in here by their   *
               ponytails if I have to.
                    (fumbling with slippers)
               I can take those geeky husbands of
               theirs any day. Both of 'em at the   *
               same time, even.

Cheryl's played nicey nice long enough. She grabs Stephen
by his pajama top, throws him back into bed. The shirt
rips.

                         CHERYL
               Lie down and shut up. Want to ruin
               the most important weekend of your
               daughter's life?

Stephen attempts escape - some MOANING and GROANING of his   *
own - but Cheryl has him pinned down.   *

He continues squirming and thrusting violently - the   *
headboard SLAMMING against the wall - loudly, rhythmically. *

8   INT. KRISTIN'S ROOM - NIGHT   8

Mike and Kristin pause in their erotic endeavors. They   *
listen to what sounds suspiciously like sexual activity
coming from their parent's bedroom.

9   INT. CARRIE-ANN'S ROOM - NIGHT   9

Carrie-Ann and Walter also stop their intermingling and
look at each other in disbelief.

10   INT. MASTER BEDROOM - NIGHT   10 *

Stephen breaks free and bolts for the door.

Cheryl leaps from the bed and tackles him to the floor.

11   INT. CARRIE-ANN'S ROOM - NIGHT   11

We hear the loud THUMP from Stephen and Cheryl's room,
followed by a series of GIGGLES and muffled conversation.

Carrie-Ann is impressed. She smiles big.

But the parental excitement has the opposite effect on
Walter. She scrambles to regain his attention.

12   INT. MASTER BEDROOM - NIGHT   12 *

Stephen is face down, crawling on his belly toward the
door.

Cheryl has him by the ankles, dragging him backwards.

                    CHERYL
          God Damn it!

She drops to the floor and starts tickling him. Stephen
can't take it, lets out a series of short, GRUNT like
giggles.

                    CHERYL
          Are you going to stop?

                    STEPHEN
          No.

She takes it up a notch. More tickles, pinches and pokes.

                    STEPHEN
          No. No. No.

                    CHERYL
              (loudly)
          Yes. Yes. Yes.

REVISED - 3/29/06 (Blue)   6.

13   INT. KRISTIN'S ROOM - NIGHT   13

Kristin and Mike lie on their backs staring out ... libidos
long gone.

                    MIKE
          Gonna be a real nice wedding.

                    KRISTIN
          Should be.

                    MIKE
          Did you pack my navy blue socks?

14   INT. CARRIE-ANN'S ROOM - NIGHT   14

Walter has found the courage to continue on, but ...

                    CARRIE-ANN
          I love you, baby.

No response.

                    CARRIE-ANN
          Hello?

                    WALTER
          Sorry.

Another MOAN is heard from the adjoining room.

                    WALTER
          I love you too.

15   INT. MASTER BEDROOM - NIGHT   15

Through great effort, Stephen has made his way to the door.

He hangs on the doorknob - half his body bent under Cheryl. *

He turns and jiggles the handle desperately.

                    CHERYL
          Don't! Stop! I swear to God, if you
          turn that handle one more time I'll
          take a chunk right out of your ass.

Stephen pauses a moment, considering.

                    STEPHEN
          You're bluffing.

                                        (CONTINUED)

15   CONTINUED: 15

He turns the handle, starts to open door.

Cheryl instantly sinks her canines into Stephen's fleshy
ass. She GROWLS and GROANS orgasmically.

Pure disbelief, coupled with tremendous pain, registers on
Stephen's contorted face.

                         STEPHEN
            Oh, dear God!   *

16   SERIES OF SHOTS   16 *

Stephen's "Godly" moment echoes throughout the house:

A) Empty kitchen.

B) Empty living room.

C) Empty hallway.

17   OMIT   17

18   INT. CARRIE-ANN'S ROOM - NIGHT   18

Silence.

Carrie-Ann and Walter lie with their backs to each other,
pillows folded around their heads - Walter with an   *
intrigued, then contemplative expression.

19   INT. KRISTIN'S ROOM - NIGHT   19

Kristin and Mike are hidden underneath the covers.

Beat.

                         MIKE
            I gotta take a leak.

20   INT. MASTER BEDROOM - NIGHT   20

Stephen rubs his wound, his back to Cheryl, who sits on the
floor trying desperately not to laugh.

A big exhale, then Stephen turns the doorknob.

                                             (CONTINUED)

REVISED - 3/29/06 (Blue)   8.
20 CONTINUED: 20

                              CHERYL
                   Stephen, please? Don't?

     Another beat before he turns to her, smiles amiably.

                              STEPHEN
                   Just need to grab an ice pack for my
                   ass, sweetie. I'll be right back.

     Cheryl smiles sheepishly as Stephen turns to go.

21 INT. HALLWAY - OFF MASTER BEDROOM - NIGHT   21

     Stephen, in ripped and torn pajamas, closes the door behind
     him and limps down the hallway.

22 ANGLE ON STAIRWAY   22

     Mike, heading upstairs, spots Stephen, does an immediate   *
     180 but then pauses, decides to forge ahead.   *

     They share an awkward moment in passing. A few steps more
     until they both turn and look over their shoulders.

     Mike nods in recognition of Stephen's talent.

     Stephen's confused, but half-smiles anyway, rubbing his
     ass.

                              STEPHEN
                   Need some ice.

     Mike just nods and shrugs as if to say, "Of course, who
     wouldn't," and then crosses into the bedroom.   *

     Stephen continues on, then glances back once more, puzzled.

     The sound of a DOOR unlatching and opening.   *

23 ANGLE ON CARRIE-ANN'S DOOR   23

     Out pops Walter's head, then the rest of his body when he   *
     confirms it's Stephen.

     He scampers on tip-toes after him.   *

                              WALTER   *
                         (quietly)   *
                   Psst.   *

REVISED - 3/29/06 (Blue)   9.

24 ANGLE ON STAIRS   24 *

Stephen, near the bottom of the stairs, pauses, then turns   *
hesitantly ...   *

But no one's there. Where once Walter was leaning over the *
railing, he's long-gone now, moving toward the stairway.   *

Stephen turns to go.   *

25 INT. STAIRWELL LANDING - NIGHT   25

Walter hurries downstairs.   *

                        WALTER   *
            Mr. B.   *

Stephen halts. There's no mistaking - it's Walter.   *

Walter draws close to Stephen, perhaps a bit too close as   *
Stephen takes a step back.   *

An awkward beat as they both just stand there in silence.   *

                        WALTER
            Mr. Baskings, I know this is terribly
            inappropriate, and doubly   *
            embarrassing, but I just wanted to say   *
            ... thank you.   *

Stephen raises an eyebrow, awaits more information.

                        WALTER
            I, ah, I hope 30, 40 years from now   *
            Carrie-Ann and I are as passionate for
            each other as you and Mrs. Baskings
            are.

A confused beat ... lingering until suddenly a big, bright, *
blinding light switches on in Stephen's brain. He starts
to correct the misunderstanding, but -
                        WALTER
            You inspire me, Sir.
                 (pause)
            Bravo.

Walter hugs Stephen.   *

Stephen, at a loss, gives Walter an apprehensive pat on the *
back, then they separate.   *

                                        (CONTINUED)

REVISED - 3/29/06 (Blue)   10.
25 CONTINUED: 25

    Walter bolts upstairs.   *

    Stephen, still a bit stunned, looks upstairs toward his   *
    closed bedroom door.   *

    A brief beat before he smiles big, turns and continues on   *
    toward the kitchen, rubbing his wounded ass.   *

26 OMIT   26

                                         FADE OUT.

Appendix E

A Filmmaker's Dozen: Thirteen Short Films Every Filmmaker Should See

"The Red Balloon" ("Le Ballon rouge")

- France, 1956
- 34 minutes
- Written and directed by Albert Lamorisse

A boy and his magical balloon endure opposition from everyone they meet as they spend their days on the streets of Paris. A classic of visual storytelling.

In 1957, "The Red Balloon" became the only short film ever to win the Academy Award for Best Original Screenplay (in competition with four feature-length films).

Available on DVD and VHS (Homevision).

"An Occurrence at Owl Creek Bridge" ("La Rivière du hibou")

- France, 1962
- 28 minutes
- Written and directed by Robert Enrico
- Based on the short story by Ambrose Bierce

During the Civil War, an accused Confederate spy finds himself at the end of a Union Army hangman's noose, but still he has dreams of escaping. Although made as an independent short in France, "An Occurrence at Owl

Creek Bridge" was eventually broadcast as an episode of the television series *The Twilight Zone*, the only episode not created by Rod Serling specifically for the series.

Academy Award for Best Short Subject, Live Action, 1964.

Available on DVD in *The Twilight Zone—Season Five—The Definitive Edition* (Image Entertainment).

"La Jetée"

- France, 1962
- 28 minutes
- Written and directed by Chris Marker

In the aftermath of World War III, survivors of an annihilated Paris live underground in the Palais de Chaillot galleries. The story is told through voiceover and a series of still photographs with only one moving image in the entire film. Don't try this at home.

Available on DVD in *Short Cinema Journal 1:2—Dreams* (PolyGram Entertainment).

"Life Lessons"

- United States, 1989
- 44 minutes
- Written by Richard Price
- Directed by Martin Scorsese

A middle-aged artist struggles with his painting and his young female assistant, who wants out of his life. Well-observed and realistically drawn characters in some unforgettable moments. Arguably, this dramatic comedy is as good as any feature film directed by Martin Scorsese or written by Richard Price.

Available on DVD in the short film anthology *New York Stories* (Walt Disney Video).

"Black Rider" ("Schwarzfahrer")

- Germany, 1993
- 12 minutes
- Written and directed by Pepe Danquart

In just twelve minutes, this film tackles the huge theme of intolerance toward immigrants in a country with only a recent history of multiculturalism. It features what may be the most expected and satisfying climax to any short film ever.

Academy Award for Best Short Film, Live Action, 1994.

Available on DVD in *Short Cinema Journal 1:1—Invention* (PolyGram Entertainment).

"Franz Kafka's It's a Wonderful Life"

- United Kingdom, 1993
- 23 minutes
- Written and directed by Peter Capaldi

Franz Kafka writes *The Metamorphosis* and discovers the true meaning of Christmas. A memorable black comedy with some truly inspired ideas, including Jiminy the Cockroach.

Academy Award for Best Short Film, Live Action, 1995.

Available on DVD in *Franz Kafka's It's a Wonderful Life…and Other Strange Tales* (Vanguard Cinema).

"Kom"

- Sweden, 1995
- 5 minutes
- Written and directed by Marianne O. Ulrichsen

Love is eternal…and this film needs just five minutes to show it. Sweet and touching, "Kom" is an impressive example of economy of expression.

Available on DVD in *Short Cinema Journal 1:4—Seduction* (PolyGram Entertainment).

"A Guy Walks into a Bar"

- United States, 1997
- 28 minutes
- Written by Carmen Elly, Roderick Plummer, and Gene Swift
- Directed by Carmen Elly

Josh Cohen heads west to become an actor and discovers that he's not in Ohio anymore. A smart and amusing mix of genres with an unusual structure that fractures time. Made as a student film at the American Film Institute in Los Angeles.

Available on DVD in *Short Cinema Journal 1:2—Dreams* (PolyGram Entertainment).

"Tunnel of Love"

- United Kingdom, 1997
- 12 minutes
- Written and directed by Robert Milton Wallace

A down-at-the-heels motorcyclist meets the woman of his dreams…if he can just catch up to her in her Mercedes-Benz. Great visual storytelling with some impressive motorcycle-mounted camerawork and a gotcha! ending.

Available on DVD in *Short Cinema Journal 1:4—Seduction* (PolyGram Entertainment).

"true."

- United States, 1999
- 3 minutes
- Written and directed by Charles Stone III

Just a bunch of friends sitting around, chilling, and wondering, "Whazzup?" Hilarious with clever, understated performances and some eye-popping editing. This film was the inspiration for a very successful series of Budweiser commercials.

Available on DVD in *Short Cinema Journal 1:8—Vision* (PolyGram Entertainment).

"Dog" ("Inja")

- ▪ Australia-South Africa, 2001
- ▪ 17 minutes
- ▪ Written and directed by Steve Pasvolsky

A powerful examination of the complex relationship between an Afrikaner farmer and his young black employee during and after Apartheid. Vividly told almost entirely through images. The open ending will keep you thinking for a long time to come.

Nominated for an Academy Award, Best Short Film, Live Action, 2003.

Available on DVD in *75th Annual Academy Awards Presents Short Films.*

"I'll Wait for the Next One" ("J'attendrai le suivant")

- ▪ France, 2002
- ▪ 4 minutes
- ▪ Written by Thomas Gaudin and Philippe Orreindy
- ▪ Directed by Philippe Orreindy

On the Paris Metro, a lonely woman meets a man looking for love—or is he? Funny and poignant. At first, you'll laugh at the unexpected climax, but, a split second later, you'll be struck by the utter sadness of it.

Nominated for an Academy Award, Best Short Film, Live Action, 2003.

Available on DVD in *75th Annual Academy Awards Presents Short Films.*

"Gridlock" ("Fait d'hiver")

- Belgium, 2002
- 6 minutes
- Written by Johan Verschueren
- Directed by Dirk Beliën

When you call home in the middle of the day, make sure that you've dialed the right number. A black comedy told with great wit and economy—just three locations and three speaking roles. The climax will leave you laughing for the rest of the day.

Nominated for an Academy Award, Best Short Film, Live Action, 2003.

Available on DVD in *75th Annual Academy Awards Presents Short Films.*

Index